D1548324

George Gordon Meade and
the War in the East

CIVIL WAR CAMPAIGNS AND COMMANDERS SERIES

Under the General Editorship of Grady McWhiney

PUBLISHED

George Gordon Meade and
the War in the East

Ethan S. Rafuse

MᴄWʜɪɴᴇʏ Fᴏᴜɴᴅᴀᴛɪᴏɴ Pʀᴇss
MᴄMᴜʀʀʏ Uɴɪᴠᴇʀsɪᴛʏ
Aʙɪʟᴇɴᴇ, Tᴇxᴀs

Cataloging-in-Publication Data

Rafuse, Ethan Sepp, 1968-
　　George Gordon Meade and the War in the East / Ethan S. Rafuse.
　　p. cm. -- (Civil War campaigns and commanders series)
　　Includes bibliographical references and index.
　　ISBN 1-893114-36-8 (cloth) -- ISBN 1-893114-37-6 (paper)
　　1. Meade, George Gordon, 1815-1872. 2. Meade, George Gordon,
1815-1872--Military leadership. 3. Generals--United States--
Biography.
4. United States. Army--Biography. 5. United States. Army of the
Potomac--Biography. 6. United States--History--Civil War,
1861-1865--Campaigns. 7. Strategy--History--19th century. I. Title.
II. Series.
　　E467.1.M38R34 2003
　　973.7'3'092--dc21

2003008422
CIP

McMurry Station, Box 637
Abilene, TX 79697-0637

Printed in the United States of America

ISBN: 1-893114-36-8
10 9 8 7 6 5 4 3 2 1

Book Designed by Rosenbohm Graphic Design

All inquiries regarding volume purchases of this book should be addressed
to McWhiney Foundation Press, McMurry Station, Box 637,
Abilene, TX 79697-0637.
Telephone inquiries may be made by calling (325) 793-4682
www.mcwhiney.org

ACKNOWLEDGMENTS

Thanks go first and foremost to my wife Rachel for her love, encouragement, and good sense, without which no project I have undertaken in the past decade could have been completed. My work on this study benefited immeasurably from the support I received from the members of the U.S. Military Academy's History Department. It has been a real pleasure to work under the direction of Department Head Robert A. Doughty and Military Division chiefs Lance A. Betros and Matthew Moten. As my officemate, Samuel J. Watson was a reliable and welcome source of prodding and advice. Matthew D. Morton's efforts, not least his making it possible for me to observe cadet field training at Camp Buckner, have done much to make my experience at West Point both personally and professionally rewarding. Charles R. Bowery Jr.'s enthusiasm and encyclopedic knowledge of the Civil War helped make the staff rides of the Virginia, Pennsylvania, and Maryland battlefields we developed and led together awesome learning experiences for me, as well as for the cadets, two of whom, Joshua Dejournett and Daniel Lawton, deserve special mention for their efforts. Joseph L. Harsh, Herman Hattaway, Carol Reardon, Brooks D. Simpson, and Steven E. Woodworth were invaluable and much appreciated sources of advice and inspiration. I also thank Glenn Dromgoole, Kevin Brock, and Robert Pace for their roles in transforming the original manuscript into publishable form, and Nathaniel Dossman for his excellent work on the biographical sketches. Finally, for their consistent support for my work and many other reasons, I dedicate this book to my parents.

To Robert and Diane Rafuse

CONTENTS

CAMPAIGNS AND COMMANDERS SERIES

Map Key

Geography

 Trees

 Marsh

 Fields

 Strategic Elevations

 Rivers

Tactical Elevations

)|(Fords

 Orchards

 Political Boundaries

Human Construction

)(Bridges

 Railroads

 Tactical Towns

● ○ Strategic Towns

□ ■ Buildings

✝ Church

 Roads

Military

 Union Infantry

 Confederate Infantry

 Cavalry

ılı Artillery

⚑ Headquarters

 Encampments

 Fortifications

 Permanant Works

 Hasty Works

 Obstructions

 Engagements

 Warships

Gunboats

Casemate Ironclad

Monitor

 Tactical Movements

 Strategic Movements

Maps by
Donald S. Frazier, Ph.D.
Abilene, Texas

MAPS

BIOGRAPHICAL SKETCHES

George Gordon Meade and
the War in the East

INTRODUCTION

Around 3:00 A.M. on June 28, 1863, Col. James A. Hardie arrived at the headquarters of Maj. Gen. George Gordon Meade, commander of the Army of the Potomac's Fifth Corps, just outside Frederick, Maryland. The previous week had been a very rough one for the general, his corps, and the entire Union army. A few weeks earlier, Robert E. Lee, fresh from his spectacular victory at Chancellorsville, had decided to once again lead his magnificent Army of Northern Virginia north of the Potomac River in pursuit of a decisive battlefield victory in enemy territory. With a considerable nudge from Pres. Abraham Lincoln and General in Chief Henry W. Halleck, Maj. Gen. Joseph Hooker had managed to get his Army of the Potomac extricated from its position north of the Rappahannock River and headed north in pursuit of the Confederates. Lee, however, enjoyed a considerable head start, which compelled the Federal army to make punishing marches under a blazing late June sun just to get within striking distance. When Hardie arrived, an exhausted Meade was getting some badly needed sleep in his tent.

Although he refused to disclose the reason for his visit, Hardie persuaded Meade's staff to allow him to see their commander. Hardie entered Meade's tent, awoke the general, and informed him that he had brought trouble from Washington. Meade naturally became quite alarmed. Like almost all of the Army of the Potomac's corps commanders, he considered Hooker a low-level braggart and intriguer who had secured his position primarily through his ability to ingratiate himself with politicians and play to their military ignorance and anti–West Point prejudices. And in the month and a half since the ignominious defeat at Chancellorsville, Meade had made little effort to conceal his growing disgust with Hooker's performance in command.

The growing friction in his relationship with Hooker had especially been manifest during a meeting between the two men shortly after Chancellorsville. According to Brig. Gen. Alexander Webb, who was present, at some point during their conversation, Hooker suggested that the blame for the defeat somehow rested with Meade. At this, Meade abandoned the restraint he had displayed toward his commanding general until then and unleashed his full temper, which was already notorious throughout the army and led some of the troops to refer to him as "a damned old goggle-eyed snapping turtle." According to Webb, "Meade talked very plainly, and getting mad, damned Hooker very freely; so much so that [I] cleared out and called off the rest of the staff, fearing that a court martial might ensue." In his letter to his wife that night, Meade proclaimed, "the *entente cordiale* is destroyed between us, and I don't regret it, as it makes me more independent and free."[1]

Consequently, Meade's first thought as Hardie stood there in his tent in the early morning of June 28 "was that he [Meade] was to be taken to Washington in arrest." The news, he later joked in a rare flash of humor, was much worse. The general was told he was the new commander of the Army of the Potomac. Meade tried to turn down the command. He complained that he had no real sense of the overall military situation and that in any case he believed First Corps commander Maj. Gen. John Reynolds was better suited to the position. Hardie, however, made it clear that the administration had made its decision and would not accept "no" for an answer. Meade resigned himself to his fate. "Well," he remarked, "I've been tried and condemned without a hearing, and I suppose I shall have to go to execution."[2]

Even though he would go on to defeat Robert E. Lee at the epic battle of Gettysburg, Meade has long suffered from a perception that he was simply the last of the Army of the Potomac commanders whose feckless conduct of operations was the main source of Union frustrations in Virginia and compelled Abraham Lincoln to bring in Lt. Gen. Ulysses S. Grant from the West in order to achieve victory. This study has a twofold purpose. First, it seeks to provide a chronicle of the life and career of the general who won the battle of Gettysburg and played a conspicuous role in several other major Civil War campaigns. Second, it will delineate the forces that shaped the Union war effort in the East and the military and political problems Army of the Potomac generals encountered as they pursued victory.

Meade's career during the Civil War is largely the story of the fundamental conflict that emerged early in the war between West Point–trained officers like Meade, who came to dominate the Army of the Potomac high command during the tenure of the army's first commander, Maj. Gen. George B. McClellan, and civilian authorities in Washington. Conflict between generals and politicians over the management of military affairs has been, of course, an enduring theme in American military history, but it was perhaps at no time more bitter than during the Civil War. This was partially a consequence of the fact that before the war, a generation of officers had, as a consequence of their experiences as cadets at West Point and as junior officers in the regular army, developed a belief that society should defer to the judgment of military professionals in the conduct of war, a corollary of which was an acute distaste for political interference—real or perceived—in military matters. The suspicion with which regular-army officers viewed Washington strategists was fully reciprocated. Many politicians early on developed an intense distaste for McClellan and the pretensions and insensitivity to political concerns they believed existed among the clique of West Point–trained officers he favored. They considered moral and personal character, manifest in a willingness to take risks and fight battles, rather than technical expertise, the test of military leadership and were impatient for results.

Although by no means the only source of civil-military tensions during the war, perhaps no dispute between the "McClellan clique" and Washington was as significant in shaping the conflict in the East (and Meade's career) as that over what line of operations Federal forces would adopt in Virginia. Meade, like his fellow professional officers, concluded in early 1862 that logistical and tactical considerations made the James River by far the Army of the Potomac's best operational option. Yet Washington strategists, motivated in large part by political considerations and a concern for public perceptions, that summer eliminated the James River option and thereafter compelled the Army of the Potomac to conduct operations along the overland route between Washington and Richmond. A variety of factors, however, would make it almost impossible to achieve decisive operational and tactical victories over the brilliant Robert E. Lee along that line. As a consequence, Meade's career as commander of a division, corps, and finally the Army of the Potomac would be the story of an exceedingly able professional officer who, though able to achieve victory in the Civil War's most famous battle, was doomed to frustration by an operational approach he knew was flawed but was unable to convince a hostile civilian authority to change.

1
CADIZ TO DETROIT

Affluence and luxury abounded in the home in Cadiz, Spain, where George Gordon Meade spent the first months of his life. Despite the distraction of the Napoleonic wars that had just come to an end when his son, the future general, was born on December 31, 1815, Philadelphia merchant Richard Worsam Meade had found Spain to be a highly favorable place to build on the considerable fortune he had inherited from his father. In 1816, however, the Spanish government imprisoned him over a series of disputes involving his finances. Fortunately, by then his wife, Margaret, had already returned to Philadelphia with their children. When Richard Meade's release was finally secured through the diplomatic efforts of the U.S. government in 1820, George was already attending school in Philadelphia. The young Meade's performance in his studies at the American Classical and Military Lyceum just outside the city inspired his father to think that he might do well at the U.S. Military Academy. Unfortunately, Richard Meade died in June 1828, three years before Pres. Andrew Jackson would approve his son's appointment to West Point.

When Meade entered West Point in 1831, the military academy was under the firm direction of Sylvanus Thayer. During the fourteen years since his appointment as superintendent, Thayer had transformed the academy from a relatively insignificant school into an institution that, for its graduates, "inspired institutional loyalties and common modes of behavior, and contributed to the development of a distinctive military subculture before the Civil War."[1] The "Thayer system" did this by subjecting cadets to an intensive four-year program of strict regimentation, constant discipline, and a highly technical curriculum that placed particular emphasis on engineering and fortification. Those who managed to survive their West Point experience developed a sense of belonging to a special class in American society—that of the professional officer.

Among the elements of the professional ethic developed among West Point–educated officers during the decades before the Civil War was contempt for politicians and an idealist vision of civil-military relations. Viewing themselves as servants of the nation (rather than of a particular party or faction) whose job it was to implement policy, professional officers believed it was their duty to steer clear of the unsavory world of politics and leave policy to the politicians. In return, they believed that politicians, who could not hope to understand the complexities of warfare that necessitated a lifetime of professional study, must acknowledge and defer to their expertise in military affairs. To their distress, however, Meade and his fellow West Pointers would consistently find that this was not a vision shared by politicians in a nation that idealized the citizen-soldier, believed the "natural" talents of the common man provided all the means necessary for military success, and had a longstanding antipathy toward standing armies.

Despite being one of the youngest cadets in his class, Meade did well in his studies at West Point. This enabled him to offset a penchant for picking up demerits and finish nineteenth of fifty-six in the Class of 1835. Commissioned a brevet second lieutenant in July of that year, he was first assigned to Company C, 3d U.S. Artillery. After a few months' training in New York, Meade and his command headed to Florida to participate in the Second Seminole War.

The young lieutenant quickly became bored with army life, however. Consequently, in October 1836, hoping to cash in on a land boom in Florida, Meade resigned his commission. He soon found work as a railroad surveyor, but the Panic of 1837 quickly dashed whatever hopes he had of striking it rich. Meade spent the next few years engaged in various surveying projects while trying to secure reappointment in the army as a topographical engineer.

Fortunately, he found an excellent ally in this endeavor. On December 31, 1840, he married Margaret Sergeant, the oldest daughter of John Sergeant, a prominent Philadelphia Whig politician with whom the Meade family had a longstanding relationship. Margaret also happened to be the sister-in-law of Congressman Henry Wise of Virginia. With their assistance, in May 1842 Meade was able to return to the army at his old rank of second lieutenant.

Although initially delighted to be back in the service and satisfied with his work as a topographical engineer, it did not take long for Meade to once again become frustrated, particularly with the slow pace of advancement in the antebellum army. But in 1846 the opportunity for adventure and the potential for promotion came with the outbreak of war with Mexico. Meade performed exceptionally as Maj. Gen. Zachary Taylor's senior topographical engineer during the first campaign of the war in northern Mexico and was cited for his performance in the general's official reports. This immensely pleased Meade, as did the spectacular scenery and the sense of adventure service in Mexico provided.

After participating in the capture of Monterrey, Meade was ordered south to Tampico to join the army Maj. Gen. Winfield Scott was planning to lead in a campaign against Mexico City. But upon reaching Scott's army, Meade found that the general's staff was already well-stocked with topographic engineers. Consequently, he was ordered to Washington and did not get to participate in Scott's triumphant campaign to the Halls of Montezuma. Thus, despite his excellent service with Taylor, there would be no promotion for Lieutenant Meade.

Yet like most West Point–trained officers, during his service in Mexico, Meade quickly manifested an intense distaste for the volunteer soldiers with whom he came into contact. "They are perfectly ignorant of discipline," he disgustedly complained to his wife after his first few weeks of working with the volunteers, "a most disorderly mass, who will give us, I fear, more trouble than the enemy. Already are our guard-houses filled daily with drunken officers and men. . . . They rob and steal the cattle and corn of the poor farmers, and in fact act more like a body of hostile Indians than of civilized whites. Their own officers have no command or control over them."[2] He was particularly disturbed by the outrages such citizen-soldiers regularly committed against Mexican civilians, not just on moral grounds but also because he feared they might provoke a popular uprising that would severely complicate military operations.

Exposure to such soldiers reinforced two elements of Meade's outlook on military affairs: a belief in the value of a strong regular army under professional leadership and a contempt for the shortsightedness of politicians when it came to military matters. "This is the miserable economy of our Government," he lamented. "It will not keep a regular army in proportion to our population and frontier, and equivalent to the wants of the country, for fear of the expense, yet six months of this volunteer force will cost as much as five years for a regular force of equal size. . . . As it is, we shall have some twenty or thirty thousand irregulars, whose usefulness may well be doubted, from past experience . . . and at an expense sufficient to have maintained the regular force for many years."[3]

Pres. James Polk's practice of granting commissions to politically connected but militarily ignorant friends further antagonized Meade. He proclaimed himself and his fellow officers absolutely mortified to see Polk, whom they believed with some justification was "prejudiced against West Point and the army," appoint to high rank individuals who had previously been dismissed from the army or the military academy "for utter inefficiency and incapacity."[4]

After returning to the United States, Meade spent the rest of the antebellum period engaged in surveying work. During the 1850s, his most extended assignment involved work on the Great Lakes survey. Although congressional funding for the project was rarely generous, Meade derived great satisfaction from this assignment. With his operations based in Detroit, where during this period he and his wife raised four children, Meade traveled extensively throughout the Old Northwest carrying out his work. By 1861, he had attained the rank of captain.

Then in April of that year, news arrived that the U.S. garrison at Fort Sumter had been attacked and forced to surrender by military forces operating under the authority of the newly born Confederate States of America. A wave of patriotic fervor swept through Detroit, and crowds quickly formed to swear allegiance to the Union and resolve to put down treason by force. Although somewhat dismayed by the fiery rhetoric with which Northern Unionists expressed their views and well aware that two of his sisters would go South with their husbands, Meade had no difficulty determining what his course would be now that civil war had begun.

2
ARMY OF THE POTOMAC

The first four months of the Civil War were extremely frustrating ones for Captain Meade. Although he deeply desired an important command, he found himself stuck in Michigan as spring turned to summer and Union armies marched southward into Virginia and Missouri. In part this was because of Meade's decision not to let members of his command participate in a Union mass meeting in Detroit in April 1861, which antagonized Michigan's powerful Republican senator Zachariah Chandler. A quick trip to Washington in June to discuss his situation with the secretary of war bore no fruit. In fact it only served to exacerbate Meade's frustration as he watched civilians and men who had been junior to him in the old army receive high ranks in the volunteer service.

Ironically, given his intense personal distaste for political meddling in such areas, Meade would eventually succeed in his quest for what he considered an appropriate rank and command thanks in large part to political connections. In the aftermath of the Union disaster at First Manassas on July 21, Sen.

David Wilmot of Pennsylvania, at the urging of a friend of Mrs. Meade, decided to see what he could do for Captain Meade. Thanks in part to Wilmot's efforts, on August 31 Meade received a commission as brigadier general of volunteers. Delighted with his appointment and accompanying orders to report to Washington, he hurriedly wrapped up affairs in Detroit and rushed to the capital.

When he reached Washington, Meade found that he was just the sort of man George B. McClellan, a fellow West Pointer and Philadelphian, was looking for to help him build the Army of the Potomac. Meade and McClellan quickly developed an enduring respect for each other, rooted in part in their mutual preference for professional military leadership and operational planning based on careful calculation of logistics and terrain, their distaste for political interference in military affairs, and their conviction that the volunteers who filled the ranks of the Union army required a lot of training and constant discipline in order to be good soldiers. McClellan instructed Meade to report to Brig. Gen. George McCall, commander of the Pennsylvania Reserves, and take command of the division's second brigade, which was then encamped at Tennallytown on the Maryland side of the Potomac.

After almost a month of training, Meade's brigade and the rest of the Pennsylvania Reserves crossed Chain Bridge into Virginia to take up a new bivouac near Langley. There Meade and his command spent a relatively quiet winter, drilling in preparation for the eagerly anticipated spring campaign. To Meade's great disappointment, his brigade missed a December 20 skirmish at Dranesville, in which McCall's other two brigades won public accolades for their handsome repulse of an attack by Confederate cavalry under the command of Brig. Gen. J.E.B. Stuart.

While he waited for major operations to commence in 1862, Meade tried as best he could to steer clear of politics and politicians. Nonetheless, he found it hard to ignore how military inaction was provoking what he perceived to be unwarranted criticism of McClellan. The pressure for a precipitous advance became particularly strong in December, and by

February 1862, Meade advised his wife, the nation's leading Republican newspaper was "becoming more violent and open in its attacks on McClellan and all regular officers." Meade took comfort, however, in a belief that such voices were "in the minority," and McClellan would not "be disturbed so long as moderate and conservative views have the upper hand."[1]

By March, however, Meade could not ignore the fact that McClellan's star had lost a great deal of its luster with many members of Congress and the Lincoln administration. Worse,

GEORGE B. MCCLELLAN

Born Pennsylvania 1826; attended preparatory schools in Philadelphia; entered University of Pennsylvania in 1840, but left upon appointment to the U.S. Military Academy in 1842, from which he graduated second in the class of 1846; brevetted 2d lieutenant of engineers 1846; promoted to 2d lieutenant 1847; participated in Mexican War as part of General Winfield Scott's command; brevetted 1st lieutenant 1847 for gallant conduct at the battles of Contreras and Churubusco and captain for gallantry at the battle of Chapultepec; following the war he served as instructor of engineering at West Point for three years; translated French regulations on bayonet exercise which the U.S. Army adopted in 1852; part of expedition to explore the sources of the Red River; promoted to 1st lieutenant in 1853; chief engineer on General Persifor F. Smith's staff; examined rivers and harbors in Texas; surveyed route for railroad across the Cascade Mountains; promoted to captain in the 1st Cavalry in 1855, but never joined his regiment; appointed member of a board of officers to study the European military systems; spent a year abroad, visiting most of the principal countries as well as the theatre of operations in the Crimea; McClellan's reports received high praise; in 1857 he resigned his army commission to become chief engineer of the Illinois Central

Lincoln's decision to impose the organization of corps on the Army of the Potomac and appoint corps commanders with whom McClellan was known to have differences was a clear sign, Meade regretfully reported to his wife, "that the President is at length yielding to the immense pressure."[2] A few days later he learned that McCall's division had been attached to the newly created First Corps, led by Maj. Gen. Irvin McDowell, the luckless commander of the Federal army that had been whipped at Manassas the previous summer.

Railroad; became vice president in charge of operations in Illinois in 1858; in 1860 he moved to Cincinnati to become president of the Ohio & Mississippi Railroad; with the outbreak of the Civil War, became major general Ohio Volunteers, commanding all state troops April 1861; less than a month later, President Abraham Lincoln appointed him major general U.S. Army in command of the Department of the Ohio; led campaign into western Virginia where he was victorious at Rich Mountain July 1861; following General Irvin McDowell's defeat at First Bull Run, McClellan was selected to lead the Army of the Potomac; appointed general-in-chief of the Armies of the United States upon the retirement of General Scott November 1861; zealously worked to improve the army's organization and training; devoted himself to the reconstruction of the Army of the Potomac; his spring 1862 Peninsular Campaign ended in failure after coming within miles of Richmond; superseded as general-in-chief by General Henry Halleck; after General John Pope led the newly designated Army of Virginia to defeat at Second Bull Run, McClellan was recalled and the Army of the Potomac regained its place as the primary Eastern force; during the Maryland Campaign September 1862, he stopped General R.E. Lee's northern advance at Antietam but failed to use his superior force to advantage; failed to aggressively pursue Lee; much displeased, Lincoln removed him from command and he saw no further duty; Democratic presidential candidate opposing Lincoln 1864; after war he worked as an engineer and served as governor of New Jersey, 1878-81; died 1885; General McClellan's efforts in organizing and training the Army of the Potomac were his chief contributions. However, his seeming unwillingness to damage his creation and a general lack of aggressiveness prevented his ultimate success.

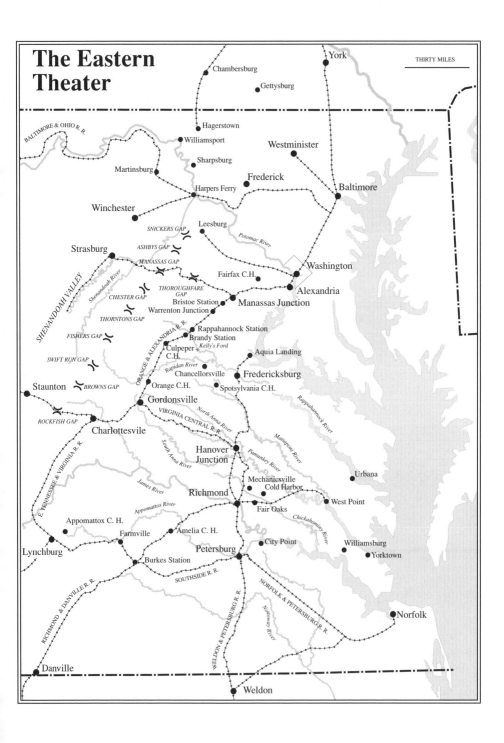

The Eastern Theater

THIRTY MILES

GEORGE McCALL

Born Philadelphia 1802; graduated U. S. Military Academy 1822, twenty-sixth out of a class of forty; brevetted 2d lieutenant assigned to 1st Infantry; transferred to 4th Infantry where he became an aide de camp for General Edmund P. Gaines; 1st Lieutenant 1829; served in Seminole Wars; Captain 1836; during the Mexican War cited for gallantry at the battles of Palo Alto and Resaca-de-la-Palma, brevetted major and then lieutenant colonel for his service there; in 1850 appointed as one of two inspectors general for the army with the staff rank of colonel; retired 1853. McCall returned to duty when the Civil War began; commissioned major general of Pennsylvania volunteers and two days later, on May 17, 1861 was commissioned a brigadier general

of U.S. volunteers by President Lincoln; commanded the "Pennsylvania Reserves" as a division in the newly created Army of the Potomac, won a small action at Dranesville, Va., in December 1861; led his division capably through severe fighting at Mechanicsville, Gaines Mill, and Glendale, where he was captured while attempting to reconnoiter his position at dusk; confined in Libby Prison until his release on August 18, 1862, exchanged for Confederate General Simon Bolivar; returned home on sick leave until he resigned on March 31, 1863; died February 26, 1868. At 60 years of age during the Peninsula Campaign, McCall was one of the eldest general officers in the Army of the Potomac.

Among the factors that contributed to the deterioration of McClellan's relationship with the president in the spring of 1862 was a fundamental disagreement over what should be done with the magnificent army the general had created. In late January McClellan presented Lincoln with a plan to put the Army of the Potomac on boats and lead it south to the lower Chesapeake Bay. From there he planned to base his operations against Richmond on one of the rivers that reached from the bay into the Virginia heartland. This document touched off a debate and contributed to the development of divisions between Washington and Army of the Potomac generals that would endure long after McClellan had left the scene.

McClellan's plan, as Meade and other West Point–trained officers in the army recognized, was grounded in an eminently sound assessment of operational and tactical realities. McClellan never had any doubt that the Army of the Potomac could carry out a successful operation against the Confederates position at Manassas once it was properly trained and organized. But the general's engineering mind gave him a keen appreciation of the power of the tactical defensive, especially if waged by troops protected by trenches and armed with modern weapons. An offensive against enemy positions at Manassas, he reasoned, would surely be costly and bloody. Moreover, even a successful offensive was unlikely to produce truly decisive results. If caught at a tactical disadvantage, any Southern commander who possessed a modicum of ability would almost always be able to decline battle if at any point his forces were at serious risk. Between Washington and Richmond, the Confederates also had plenty of room to maneuver and several excellent rivers behind which they could establish defensive positions formidable enough to inflict significant casualties on any attacking Union force. "I do not wish to waste life in useless battles," McClellan explained. "A battle gained at Manassas will result merely in the possession of the field of combat. . . . [A]t best we can follow it up but slowly . . . for [the enemy] could fall back upon other positions, & fight us again & again." This would make the conflict in Virginia "a very difficult and tedious matter," he argued, one that might "require years of warfare & expenditure" of blood and treasure to bring to a successful end."[3]

In addition, any army marching from Washington to Richmond would have to depend on the Orange and Alexandria Railroad for supplies (no Civil War army of substantial size could operate very long if it did not possess access to either a river or railroad), at least until it reached the Rappahannock River. At that point the Orange and Alexandria's southwestward course led a Union army away from Richmond. If the Army of the Potomac wanted to continue toward the Confederate capital, it would have to move to Fredericksburg; adopt the Richmond, Fredericksburg, and Potomac Railroad as its line of operations; and advance directly south toward Richmond from there.

Such a move, however, would require crossing a series of rivers—the Rappahannock, Mattaponi, North Anna, and South Anna—that provided the Confederates with good defensive positions. It could also give the Rebels an open road to Washington beyond the Federal western flank. Then there was the problem of a railroad's vulnerability to raids. A single Rebel sympathizer with a match could disrupt traffic for days, throwing off painstakingly developed schedules for the transportation of supplies and reinforcements. Consequently, every mile the Federal army advanced south along the railroad would result in the detachment of combat troops to protect the track, while the enemy, relieved of guarding that mile, would gain in combat strength.

McClellan pointed out that all these problems could easily be avoided by basing Union operations in Virginia on the rivers that flowed into the lower Chesapeake Bay. Instead of being obstacles to a successful advance, a Federal army operating from there would find the rivers of the Virginia tidewater, especially the James, a convenient and secure means for transporting troops and supplies thanks to the North's overwhelming advantage in naval resources. Operating in conjunction with the U.S. Navy, the Army of the Potomac could make an irresistible advance along the rivers toward Richmond, using water transportation and naval gunboats to eliminate Confederate strong points or bypass them altogether. Although the falls of the James would effectively prohibit amphibious turning movements around Richmond itself, there the Federal army, with its unmatched superiority in artillery and engineering, could turn to siege operations. Not only was siege warfare something Meade and other officers who had completed the program at West Point, with its heavy emphasis on engineering, were particularly well prepared to carry out successfully, but it was also one that the Confederates—as they themselves recognized—did not possess the means to resist.

The lower Chesapeake strategy immediately appealed to the West Point–trained military professionals whom McClellan favored within his army's high command. In concept, it harkened back to the campaigns of Maurice, Comte de Saxe, the greatest practitioner of the art of limited war in the eighteenth century, in Flanders and along the Meuse River during the War of the Austrian Succession. There was no coincidence here. The "Age of Limited War" was also the "Age of Reason and Science," during which military men sought to isolate warfare from public opinion and limit the effects of war to armies and avoid unnecessarily antagonizing the civilian population. Freed from considerations for public opinion, generals felt free to conduct campaigns purely on the basis of technical skill and the application of "scientific principles" that restrained the destructiveness of war and made it a carefully calculated tool for achieving political goals.

President Lincoln, however, immediately objected to the plan McClellan put forward. As he and other politicians saw it, the Army of the Potomac's mission was as much to protect Washington as it was to defeat the Rebel army and capture its capital. Sending the bulk of the army to the lower Chesapeake, Lincoln feared, might open the administration to charges that it had neglected its responsibility to completely secure the capital. Moreover, Lincoln understood that the public and politicians thought of war in terms of decisive battles determined by heroic charges on defenses by men possessing a "proper martial spirit," had no appreciation for the real problems the overland approach entailed, and had little patience for siege warfare. Unlike in absolutist Europe during the Age of Reason, warfare could not be isolated from the citizenry of the American republic. Consequently, in deciding whether or not to adopt a particular military strategy, the president had to take into account popular perceptions and how certain plans would be received by politicians and the general public.

To make matters worse, by the spring of 1862, Radical Republican politicians had developed a deep distrust of McClellan and the West Point–educated officers he brought into the army, such as Meade, John F. Reynolds, Gouverneur K. Warren, Winfield Scott Hancock, Fitz John Porter, and William B. Franklin. They rightly perceived that these men were hostile to efforts to conform military planning to political exigencies. Efforts by McClellan and others to explain the importance of lines of operations, the problem of overcoming fortifications, and the value of secure logistics to Northern politicians fell on deaf ears. Politicians had no patience for these problems or the West Point officers who had to deal with them, nor would they accept any plan of operations that did not have as their objective a battle. An overland advance from Washington would not only protect the capital but also certainly result in battle.

Despite persistent complaints by leading Republicans about McClellan and his own growing reservations about the general, Lincoln eventually let him take his army to the lower Chesapeake in March 1862—but not without thoroughly hedging his bets. In doing so Lincoln provided much ammunition to those officers who were skeptical of the wisdom and good will of the nation's political leadership when it came to military matters. The most important of these actions was Lincoln's decision to withhold McDowell's corps from the Army of the Potomac just as McClellan was beginning his campaign on the Peninsula, the land between the York and James Rivers. The president did this in order to protect Washington from what McClellan and other West Pointers correctly perceived to be a grossly exaggerated threat posed by Maj. Gen. Thomas J. "Stonewall" Jackson's small Confederate army in the Shenandoah Valley.

Consequently, instead of delivering the decisive blow at Yorktown as McClellan had planned, Meade and the rest of the First Corps found themselves guarding and repairing the Orange and Alexandria Railroad. In letters to his wife, Meade was unable to contain his anger at what he perceived as attempts by Washington politicians to destroy McClellan by compromising his campaign. "It is gross injustice to McClellan

WILLIAM B. FRANKLIN

Born Pennsylvania 1823; graduated U.S. Military Academy 1843, first in his class of forty-three that included U.S. Grant; brevetted 2d lieutenant assigned to engineers; part of Great Lakes survey team 1843–45; with  Philip Kearney's Rocky Mountain expedition 1846; won two brevets for Mexican War service, including one for gallantry at Buena Vista; from 1848 to 1861 he was involved in numerous engineering projects, among these was the construction of a new dome for the national capitol; taught engineering at West Point; gained slow but steady promotion reaching captain in 1857; at the outbreak of the Civil War he was commissioned colonel of the 12th U.S. Infantry and brigadier general U.S. Volunteers shortly thereafter; commanded a brigade at First Bull Run and a division in the Washington defenses following that debacle; commanded a division and then the Sixth Corps during the Peninsular Campaign; promoted to major general U.S. Volunteers July 1862; directed the Sixth Corps during the Maryland Campaign and was conspicuously involved at Crampton's Gap, South Mountain, and Antietam, September 1862; commanded the Left Grand Division at Fredericksburg, after which he was accused by General Ambrose Burnside of failing to follow orders; although not disciplined, his career was irreparably damaged; sent West, he commanded the Nineteenth Corps in General N.P. Banks's Red River Expedition during which he was twice wounded, ending his field service; brevetted brigadier general U.S. Army for his actions in the Peninsular Campaign and major general U.S. Army for war service, he was retired in 1866; from then until 1888, he was an executive with Colt's Firearms Manufacturing Company; he also supervised the construction of the Connecticut state capitol and held a variety of public offices until his death at Hartford in 1903. Although he owned a relatively solid service record, General Franklin could not overcome the stigma of the disaster at Fredericksburg.

to interrupt and interfere with his plans," Meade remarked. "How a man can been expected to carry on a campaign when such interferences and derangement of plans are perpetrated, surpasses my comprehension. . . . God grant that he may be victorious and preserved, that he may outlive and put down his enemies!"[4]

Meade nonetheless remained confident that McClellan would overcome the difficulties the politicians had thrown in front of him. Moreover, Meade's approval of the decision to operate from the lower Chesapeake received confirmation from an April 13 inspection of the formidable (and now abandoned) works the Confederates had constructed at Centerville and Manassas. He also, from firsthand observation, gained a great appreciation during this time of the awesome logistical and operational problems the army would have encountered had it tried to conduct a major campaign north of Richmond, whether along the Orange and Alexandria or from Fredericksburg.

Finally, on June 9 Lincoln relented to McClellan's demand that at least part of McDowell's corps be released for operations on the Peninsula. Although immensely pleased that his brigade was part of that reinforcement, Meade arrived on the Peninsula angry at the wasted weeks north of Richmond, during which he saw more than enough to confirm his suspicions regarding the good faith and military judgment of the nation's political leaders. "You see how completely Jackson succeeded," he complained, "paralyzing McDowell's force of forty thousand men, through the stupidity of the authorities at Washington."[5]

After arriving with his portion of the Pennsylvania Reserves at White House on the Pamunkey River, where McClellan had set up his main supply base, Meade marched his men to the front line. There they went into position behind Beaver Dam Creek, north of the Chickahominy River and only a few miles from Richmond. A few days later Meade went over to McClellan's headquarters and "had a very pleasant visit." McClellan, he told his wife, "talked very freely of the way he had been treated, and said positively that had not McDowell's corps been withdrawn, he would long before now have been in Richmond."[6]

On June 26, four days after this conversation, Confederate general Robert E. Lee began his attempt to dislodge the Federal army from the gates of Richmond with an attack on the Union position at Beaver Dam Creek. Meade's brigade remained in reserve the entire fight and thus was not immediately engaged.

Although the Confederate attacks were easily and bloodily repulsed, a large force under Stonewall Jackson managed to reach a position from which it could cut the Union supply line to White House Landing. Consequently, McClellan decided to abandon the White House base and withdraw his army south through White Oak Swamp to a new base at Harrison's Landing on the James River. To buy time to complete preparations for his change of base, he instructed Fitz John Porter to pull all Union forces north of the Chickahominy back from Beaver Dam Creek the night of June 26–27 but not to cross to the south bank of the river until the following evening.

That night Meade, along with the rest of the Federal force north of the Chickahominy, fell back to a new position near Gaines's Mill. Lee kept up the pressure, and a second day of heavy fighting took place, in which the Rebels managed to achieve some tactical success but were unable to destroy Porter's force in a fierce battle. Unlike at Beaver Dam Creek, Meade personally was in the thick of the fighting at Gaines's Mill. On the night of June 27, Meade and his command crossed to the south side of the Chickahominy and began marching south toward the James. Within a few days, McCall's command had reached the vital crossroads near Glendale and established a position facing west in order to protect the Federal line of retreat along Willis Church Road.

On June 30 Lee's Confederates launched a determined attack on the Federal line near Glendale. When the Rebel assault began, Meade immediately rode to where the fighting was fiercest to personally inspire and lead his men. Soon two bullets struck him: one hit his forearm, the other entered his right side and exited above his hip. Although in intense pain,

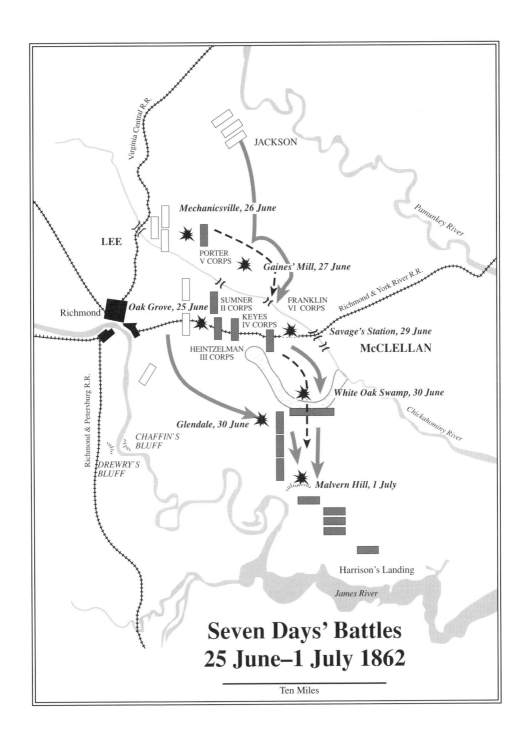

Seven Days' Battles
25 June–1 July 1862

Ten Miles

Meade calmly turned over command of the brigade to one of his regimental commanders and proceeded to a field hospital. From there he was taken to a hospital at Haxall's Landing, where surgeons patched up his wounds and put him on a boat headed north.

Meade arrived at Philadelphia on July 4 and experienced a remarkably quick recovery from his wounds. By mid-August, he was back with his command and found that the situation in Virginia had taken a new turn. Although McClellan had successfully withdrawn his army to Harrison's Landing, and in the process inflicted a severe beating on Lee's Army of Northern

HENRY W. HALLECK

Born New York 1815; Halleck was graduated from the U.S. Military Academy in 1839, third in his class of thirty-one; commissioned a 2d lieutenant of engineers, he worked on New York Harbor's fortifications and made an inspection tour of France; promoted to 1st lieutenant, he served in California during the Mexican War, earning a brevet to captain; an astute military thinker, "Old Brains," as he was called, authored *Report on the Means of National Defense* and *Elements of Military Art and Science*; he also translated Henri Jomini's *Vie Politique et Militaire de Napoleon*; promoted to the full rank of captain in 1853, Halleck resigned his commission the following year; he entered a lucrative legal practice in San Francisco, wrote two volumes on mining law, helped draft California's constitution, and was active in the state militia; with the onset of the Civil War, General Winfield Scott recommended Halleck to President Abraham Lincoln; commissioned directly into the regular army as a major general, Halleck became the fourth ranking officer in the army, following Scott, George B. McClellan, and John C. Frémont; always an effective administrator, Halleck took command of the Department of the Missouri in November

Virginia, the Lincoln administration was unwilling to give him the reinforcements he deemed necessary to resume the campaign along the James River. An exasperated administration then called Maj. Gen. Henry W. Halleck to Washington to assume the post of general in chief. Halleck, who shared Lincoln's uneasiness at making the main campaign in Virginia from the Peninsula, directed McClellan to evacuate his position along the James and send his forces to northern Virginia to assist Maj. Gen. John Pope's operations along the overland route. It was, Meade recognized to his great distress, "a virtual condemnation of all McClellan's movements."[7]

1861, succeeding Frémont, and brought much-needed order to the chaotic West; in March his command was extended and redesignated the Department of the Mississippi; much of his department's success came with the battlefield accomplishments of his subordinates, Generals U.S. Grant (Forts Henry and Donelson, Shiloh), Samuel Curtis (Pea Ridge), and John Pope (Island No. 10); Halleck, however, proved an inept field commander when, after Shiloh, he took control of Grant's army and failed to crush the badly outnumbered Rebels at Corinth; named commander in chief of U.S. forces, Halleck moved to Washington, D.C., where his role became increasingly advisory and administrative; displaced by Grant's promotion in March 1864, Halleck became chief of staff and served credibly for the balance of the war; afterward, he headed the Military Division of the James, from April to June 1865, and the Division of the Pacific until 1869, when he assumed command of the Division of the South, headquartered at Louisville, Kentucky; he died there in 1872. General Halleck was extremely unpopular among his fellow officers and members of the Lincoln Administration; he owned a poor disposition, was difficult to work with, and frequently criticized other generals; this, combined with poor leadership qualities and his demonstrated inability as a field commander, left him the target of much ridicule; but he was a fine administrator and as such contributed greatly to the Federal victory and was especially useful after Grant became commanding general.

As the Army of the Potomac began departing the Peninsula, Meade rejoined his brigade at Falmouth, just across the Rappahannock River from Fredericksburg, on August 17. There he learned the Pennsylvania Reserves had a new commander, John Fulton Reynolds, a capable and highly regarded West Pointer with whom Meade already enjoyed an excellent professional and personal relationship. Five days later the Reserves moved up the Rappahannock in search of Pope's army.

By then, however, Pope was finding out that operating along the Orange and Alexandria was no easy task, and Lee was doing everything he could to take advantage of the situation. By skillfully maneuvering his forces, the Southern general compelled Pope to retreat from the Rappahannock River and then thoroughly whipped the Federal army at the Second Battle of Manassas. Meade and his men reached the Rappahannock just in time to participate in Pope's retreat to Manassas, where on August 30 they helped preserve the Federal line of retreat after the battle had gone irretrievably against the Union.

Meade was naturally disgusted at the incredible transformation of the war since June, when McClellan had been on the Peninsula and Meade had confidently predicted the rebellion practically at an end. "We have been," he complained after Second Manassas, "outmaneuvered . . . , now we have to defend our capital, and perhaps resist an invasion of our soil through Maryland, and all from the willful blindness of our rulers."[8]

After his victory at Manassas, Lee indeed decided to cross the Potomac into Maryland, hoping to force the Union army into the field before it could recover from its defeat and to achieve a decisive victory on Northern soil that would break the North's will to continue the war. Fearful that the Confederates intended to carry the fighting into his state, Pennsylvania governor Andrew Curtin petitioned Washington for Reynolds to be relieved from command of the Reserves and ordered to Harrisburg to organize the state's militia. Authorities approved Curtin's appeal, and Meade was immediately selected as Reynolds's replacement as commander of the Pennsylvania Reserves, now officially designated the Third Division, First Corps.

In addition to his new duties, Meade also found himself serving under a new corps commander. With McDowell under intense criticism for his conspicuous role in the debacle at Second Manassas, the administration decided to replace him with Maj. Gen. Joseph Hooker, whose exploits as a division commander on the Peninsula had earned him the nickname "Fighting Joe." In addition to his handsome visage and aggressiveness on the battlefield, Hooker had also attracted the attention of influential Republican politicians in Washington for his willingness to criticize, and his independence from, the McClellan clique in the Army of the Potomac.

In response to Lee's move into Maryland, the Lincoln administration merged Pope's Army of Virginia with the Army of the Potomac and, with great reluctance, placed McClellan in command of the combined force. McClellan got his army ready for the field much faster than Lee anticipated, and by September 7 he was marching his army north and west toward Frederick, Maryland, in search of the Rebels. Meade and his division reached that town on September 13 and, early the next morning, advanced toward Turner's Gap in South Mountain, which separated McClellan's and Lee's armies. At about two in the afternoon, Meade reached the base of South Mountain. Hooker, seeing the main road through the gap blocked by forces under Confederate general Daniel Harvey Hill, ordered Meade to lead his command to the right and move up the mountain along Frostown Road.

When he reached the road, Meade opened fire with his artillery and ordered his three brigades forward, over "rocks, stone walls, and the most rugged country I almost ever saw." Hill later wrote that he realized at that point that his position at South Mountain was in serious danger, for "Meade was one of our most dreaded foes; he was always in deadly earnest, and he eschewed all trifling."[9] Despite tough resistance by the Confederate defenders, Meade's men surged up the slopes of South Mountain and overwhelmed the Rebel left, rendering Hill's position at Turner's Gap untenable.

After his defeat at South Mountain, Lee fell back to the town of Sharpsburg, where he took up a strong defensive posi-

JOSEPH HOOKER

Born Massachusetts 1814; graduated U.S. Military Academy 1837, twenty-ninth in his class of fifty cadets; brevetted 2d lieutenant assigned to artillery; on frontier duty, fought in Seminole wars, and held a staff assignment at West Point; served conspicuously in Mexican War, earning three brevets; captain 1848; resigned his commission 1853; engaged in farming in California and served as colonel in the state militia; offered his services to the Union at the outbreak of the Civil War but was initially snubbed owing to poor relations with General Winfield Scott; commissioned brigadier general U.S. Volunteers May 1861; led a division in the

Peninsular Campaign and at Second Bull Run; major general U.S. Volunteers May 1862; commanded First Corps and was wounded at Antietam September 1862; promoted brigadier general U.S. Army to date from the battle; named to command the Army of the Potomac January 1863; routed by badly outnumbered Confederates at Chancellorsville, but received the thanks of Congress for his subsequent defense of Washington May 1863; relieved at his own request in June; sent West, took command of the newly formed Twentieth Corps Army of the Cumberland, which he led with great success at Chattanooga and during the Atlanta Campaign; resigned when overlooked for the command of the Army of the Tennessee following the death of General James B. McPherson; for the balance of the war he exercised various departmental commands; brevetted major general U.S. Army for Chattanooga victory; remained in the regular army until his retirement in 1868; died 1879. Although the disaster at Chancellorsville tainted his career, General Hooker proved to be a competent combat officer at division and corps level. While he hated his sobriquet "Fighting Joe," it was nonetheless appropriate.

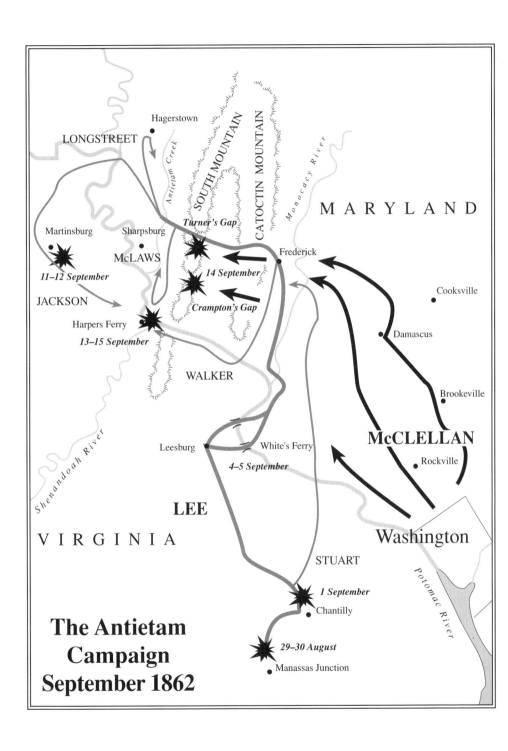

Hagerstown

LONGSTREET

SOUTH MOUNTAIN

CATOCTIN MOUNTAIN

Antietam Creek

Monocacy River

MARYLAND

Martinsburg

Sharpsburg

McLAWS

Turner's Gap

Frederick

11–12 September

14 September

Cooksville

JACKSON

Crampton's Gap

Harpers Ferry

Damascus

13–15 September

WALKER

Brookeville

McCLELLAN

Leesburg

White's Ferry

Rockville

4–5 September

LEE

VIRGINIA

Washington

STUART

Potomac River

Shenandoah River

1 September

Chantilly

**The Antietam
Campaign
September 1862**

29–30 August

Manassas Junction

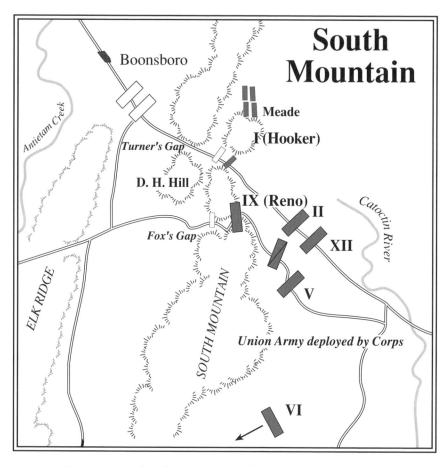

tion on a ridge between the Potomac River and Antietam Creek. McClellan, accompanied by Hooker and Meade, arrived opposite the Confederates on the afternoon of September 15 and, following a careful survey of the enemy position, decided to attack. In McClellan's battle plan Hooker's First Corps, supported by Maj. Gen. Joseph F. K. Mansfield's Twelfth Corps, would strike the Rebel left at dawn on September 17. He hoped that this attack would either overwhelm that flank or compel Lee to shift forces to prevent that from happening. If the latter occurred, it would enable an assault on the Rebel right by Maj. Gen. Ambrose Burnside's command, scheduled for later in the morning, to achieve decisive success.

After a thick morning fog lifted, Meade led his division across the Antietam on September 16 and moved into position in what would become known as the East Woods. The Federals' arrival did not go unnoticed, and a sharp firefight took place between the Reserves and Rebel skirmishers. With nightfall, the fighting died down, and Meade and his men settled into their new position as a light rain fell.

At dawn on September 17, Hooker began his attack on the Confederate left, with Brig. Gen. Abner Doubleday's division forming the corps's right and Brig. Gen. James B. Ricketts's division forming its left. Meade's division was positioned in between and given the task of advancing due south from the North Woods through a forty-acre cornfield. Hooker's advance touched off a brutal fight all along the front, as Confederate divisions under Brig. Gens. Alexander Lawton, John R. Jones, and John B. Hood greeted the Federals with heavy volleys of musketry and ferocious counterattacks. To make matters worse, Confederate horse artillery on Nicodemus Heights zeroed in on their positions and poured a deadly enfilading fire on the advancing Federals from the west. The carnage was appalling. Hooker later remarked: "every stalk of corn in the northern and greater part of the field was cut as closely as could have been done with a knife, and the slain lay in rows precisely as they had stood in their ranks. . . . It was never my fortune to witness a more bloody, dismal battlefield."[10]

Meade did the best he could to maintain order in the "Bloody Cornfield" and keep his men fighting as casualties mounted. With his saber drawn, he rode among his units, exhorting them on despite the severe, though not mortal, wounding of his favorite horse, Baldy, and a deep bruise on his thigh caused by a piece of Confederate grapeshot. Then when Hooker went down with a wounded foot, McClellan ordered Meade to assume command of the First Corps. By the time Hooker left the field, however, his command's attack was spent, and the Twelfth Corps had taken over the fight north of Sharpsburg. With its shattered ranks exhausted and running out of ammunition, Meade saw no alternative but to withdraw the First Corps north to recuperate. There it remained until

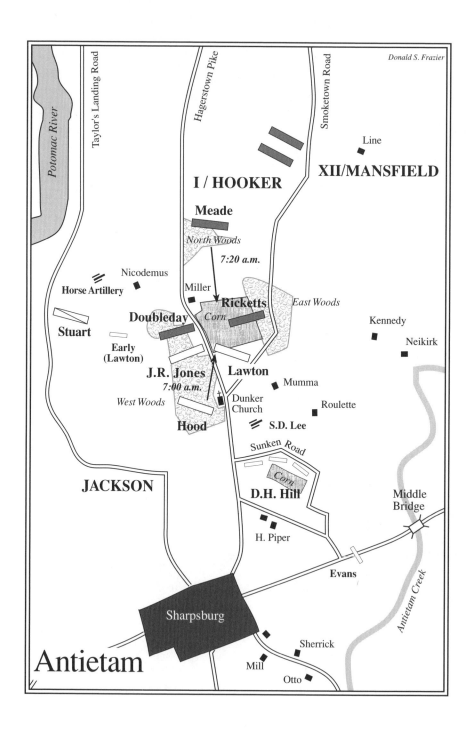

Donald S. Frazier

nightfall brought an end to the Battle of Antietam, with Lee's badly battered army still holding a compact line protecting its crossing point over the Potomac. After a day of inactivity on September 18, Lee returned to Virginia.

Despite his solid performance at Antietam, Meade's tenure as commander of the First Corps came to an end in late September when Reynolds returned to the army. Although disappointed to once again return to division command, he was glad to have his friend back. As Meade settled back into command of his division, McClellan went to work on the massive task of revitalizing the army. Among the tasks he wrestled with for over a month after Antietam were the training of thousands of raw troops, integrating them into the army, and the rehabilitation of a logistical support system that had badly deteriorated during Pope's tenure in command and had suffered from neglect on the part of the government.

Meade fully endorsed McClellan's efforts to rehabilitate the army after the rough handling it had been subjected to since August and bitterly complained to his wife about the poor support the general received from Washington for his efforts. "Everyone who returns to camp says that McClellan's position is most precarious," Meade wrote, "and that if he does not advance soon and do something brilliant he will be superseded. At the same time they do not, or will not, send from Washington the supplies absolutely necessary for us to have before we can move. I have *hundreds* of men in my command without shoes, going barefooted, and I can't get a shoe for a man or beast. . . . It is hard the army should be censured for inaction when the most necessary supplies for their movement are *withheld*."[11]

Although he himself quickly grew restless from inactivity, Meade was unable to comprehend the Lincoln administration's distress over the army's failure to resume the offensive on September 18 or during the month that followed. Unlike the politicians in Washington, he was keenly aware of how much damage the horrific bloodletting at Sharpsburg had inflicted on the army and of its need to recover mentally from such a ghastly experience. Moreover, he shared McClellan's belief that the army should take the time to rest and build up its supplies before resuming operations against Lee.

Not until October 29 would Meade's division cross the Potomac into Virginia. By November 7, his command, along with the bulk of the army, had arrived in the vicinity of Warrenton after an admirable series of marches that were a product of the care with which McClellan had taken in rebuilding and refitting it. The Lincoln administration, however, did not feel that this result was worth the time it took to bring it about and decided to remove McClellan once and for all from command of the Army of the Potomac. Ambrose Burnside was chosen as his replacement. Burnside at first tried to turn down the command but reluctantly accepted when the administration threatened to give the army to Joseph Hooker, whose loose talk, coziness with anti-McClellan elements in the capital, and constant intriguing had antagonized many in the army's officer corps.

McClellan may have been gone, but divisions over the conduct of the Union war effort in Virginia remained deep and bitter. On the one side were those division and corps commanders who respected McClellan and believed the execution of his eminently sound strategic ideas had been fatally compromised by selfish and ignorant politicians within Congress and the Lincoln administration. On the other side were those officers who, out of desire for personal gain or a sincere antagonism toward McClellan and his clique of West Pointers, had cultivated good relations with Republicans in Washington.

Meade recognized there were faults with McClellan's generalship. He agreed with the general's desire not to renew the fighting at Antietam on September 18 and his decision to take the time to rest and refit the army in the month that followed. Yet Meade also confided to his wife that he had come to the conclusion that McClellan "errs on the side of prudence and caution, and that a little more rashness on his part would improve his generalship."[12]

Still, there was no question that, when it came to the debate over what should be done in Virginia, Meade's sympathies rested firmly with McClellan and likeminded members of the Army of the Potomac high command, not with Washington. Fortunately, by the end of 1862, he had yet to achieve a position of sufficient prominence for his opinions to be of interest to Washington politicians and, thus, had been able to do his job, follow the orders given him, and lead his command as he saw fit, free from the persistent scrutiny under which other officers had labored. That would change within a few months.

3

DIVISION AND CORPS COMMAND

Whatever faults Ambrose Burnside may have possessed as a general, no one could accuse him of failing to understand that his appointment carried with it the expectation that he would undertake a major campaign before winter along the overland approach to Richmond. He promptly organized the Army of the Potomac into three "grand divisions" and marched quickly overland to Falmouth, on the north bank of the Rappahannock River across from Fredericksburg. From there he intended to cross the river and proceed south toward the Southern capital along the Richmond, Fredericksburg, and Potomac Railroad.

When, through camp scuttlebutt, Meade learned of the discussions between Burnside and Washington regarding the army's line of operations, he responded with a long, anguished letter to his wife. "McClellan," he noted with apprehension, "has always objected to operating on this line, and insisted on the James River as being the proper base for operations." General Halleck's insistence that the Army of the Potomac advance along the Orange and Alexandria was, in Meade's mind, preposterous and could only be attributed to "Washington influence." He protested: "This road has but one track : . . ; the known capacity of the road is insufficient by one-third to carry the daily supplies required for this army. This fact to an ordinarily intelligent mind, unbiased by ridiculous fears for the safety of Washington, ought to be conclusive." Burnside's plan to use the Richmond, Fredericksburg, and Potomac, Meade proclaimed, "is open to the same objection as the other, except that it is only seventy-five miles. Still it will require a larger number to protect those seventy-five miles and keep open our communications than it will to attack Richmond itself." The whole matter left him profoundly dispirited. "I must confess," he added, "this interference by politicians with military men . . . make[s] me feel very sad and very doubtful of the future."[1]

In Burnside's reorganization of the army, John Reynolds's First Corps was assigned to the Left Grand Division, commanded by Maj. Gen. William B. Franklin. After his army's rapid march from Warrenton to Falmouth, Burnside lost over a week waiting for pontoon bridges to arrive from Washington before trying to cross the Rappahannock. As the weather turned cold, Meade became deeply pessimistic regarding the army's prospects. The whole problem as he saw it, "comes from taking the wrong line of operations, the James River being the true and only practicable line of approach. . . . The blind infatuation of the authorities at Washington, sustained, I regret to say by Halleck, who as a soldier ought to know better, will not permit the proper course to be adopted." The best Meade hoped for by late November was that weather would compel the army to go into winter quarters and prevent the undertaking of operations that he feared would result in "a check, if not disaster."[2]

The army did not go into winter quarters. When the pontoon bridges finally arrived, Burnside ordered his men to cross the Rappahannock. On December 11–12, Franklin's command crossed the river downstream from Fredericksburg and moved to a point from which it could attack the Confederate right near Hamilton's Crossing. Early on the morning of the thirteenth, Meade, who only two days before had learned of his promotion to major general of volunteers, roused his 4,500 men and moved them into position to carry out their part of the attack. Burnside's plan for the day was for Franklin's command to attack the Confederate right, commanded by Lt. Gen. Stonewall Jackson, on Prospect Hill south of Fredericksburg, while Maj. Gen. Edwin Sumner's grand division hit the Rebel left just west of town. Hooker's grand division would be held in reserve to reinforce either Franklin or Sumner if necessary.

At dawn, an uneasy Meade began shelling the Confederate line with his artillery preparatory to attack. When told that the plan was for his division to make the assault supported by only one other division, he immediately protested. "The mistake of

AMBROSE EVERETT BURNSIDE

Born Indiana 1824; apprenticed to a tailor and worked in a shop until friends of his father, an Indiana legislator, secured him an appointment to the U.S. Military Academy, where he graduated eighteenth in the class of 1847; appointed 2d lieutenant in 3rd Artillery in 1847, but saw little service in Mexico; promoted to 1st lieutenant in 1851; married Mary Richmond Bishop of Rhode Island in 1852 and resigned from army a year later to manufacture a breech-loading rifle he invented; company went bankrupt in 1857; major general in the Rhode Island militia and treasurer of the Illinois Central Railroad before the Civil War; in 1861 organized and became colonel of 1st Rhode Island Infantry, which was among the earliest regiments to reach Washington; became friend of President Lincoln and received promotion to brigadier general of volunteers in August 1861 after commanding a brigade at the Battle of Bull Run; in 1862 commanded a successful operation

Antietam," he told Franklin, "was in one corps attacking at a time and here they were committing the same fault; that he had little over 4,000 men in his division, and that though he believed he could carry the heights he could not hold them." Franklin replied that he was merely following Burnside's wishes that he use "a division at least" for the attack and told him the order stood.[3]

At approximately 1:00 P.M. Meade's lead brigade, commanded by twenty-four-year-old Col. William Sinclair, crossed the Old Richmond Stage Road and began its advance over the open ground that separated the Federal and Confederate positions south of Fredericksburg. Fortunately, Meade's advance was directed right at the most vulnerable point in Jackson's line: a six-hundred-yard gap between James Lane's and James

along the North Carolina Coast; commissioned a major general of volunteers and received awards and thanks from various states; at Sharpsburg he wasted too much time crossing Antietam Creek and attacking the Confederate right; after twice declining command of the Army of the Potomac, he finally accepted, although he considered himself incompetent and proved himself correct by crossing the Rappahannock River in December 1862 and making a disastrous attack on the awaiting Confederate army at Fredericksburg; "I ought to retire to private life," Burnside informed President Lincoln, who after relieving him of command in the East assigned him to command the Department of the Ohio; at Lincoln's urging, he advanced into East Tennessee and in November 1863 repulsed an assault on Knoxville by Confederates under James Longstreet; Burnside and his Ninth Corps returned to the East in 1864 to serve under Grant from the Wilderness to Petersburg; blamed by General George Meade for the Union failure at the Crater, Burnside shortly thereafter went on leave and never returned to duty; in 1865 he resigned his commission; after the war he became president of various railroad and other companies; elected governor of Rhode Island in 1866 and reelected in 1867 and 1868; elected to U.S. Senate from Rhode Island in 1874, where he served until his death at Bristol, Rhode Island, in 1881.

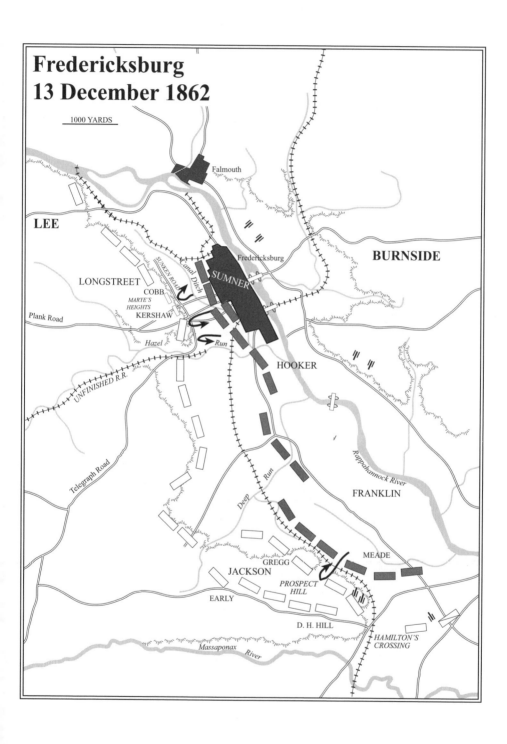

**Fredericksburg
13 December 1862**

1000 YARDS

Falmouth

LEE

Fredericksburg

BURNSIDE

LONGSTREET

COBB

MARYE'S
HEIGHTS

KERSHAW

Plank Road

SUMNER

Canal Ditch

SUNKEN ROAD

Hazel

Run

HOOKER

UNFINISHED R.R.

Telegraph Road

Deep

Run

Rappahannock River

FRANKLIN

MEADE

GREGG

JACKSON

PROSPECT
HILL

EARLY

D. H. HILL

HAMILTON'S
CROSSING

Massaponax

River

Archer's Confederate brigades. Sinclair's brigade, along with Col. Albert Magilton's and Brig. Gen. Conrad F. Jackson's, thrust into the gap and overran a thin line of Southern troops commanded by Brig. Gen. Maxcy Gregg. After securing a foothold on the military road that connected Lee's line, Meade's men quickly moved to exploit their success by turning to the left and right to further expand the breakthrough.

At this point, however, the attack began to lose steam as the rough, wooded terrain and the large number of prisoners requiring escort to the rear began to take a severe toll on the division's organization. Moreover, Meade's men quickly realized that they were alone and unsupported, for the attacks of Brig. Gen. John Gibbon's division on their right encountered much stiffer resistance and were unable to achieve a penetration. Reynolds's other division, Abner Doubleday's, had been held back at the stage road to guard the Federal left.

Meade did his best to keep his men in order and moving forward, but to no avail. It did not take long for Stonewall Jackson to rush reinforcements to the scene of Meade's breakthrough and begin pouring a terrific fire into the Federal ranks. After a number of calls to headquarters for assistance went unanswered, Meade decided to ride back to inquire personally. He quickly found Brig. Gen. David Birney and asked whether he was bringing his division from the Third Corps forward to help. When Birney stated he intended to wait for orders from Franklin before doing anything, Meade exploded with a barrage of profanity that, as one lieutenant remarked, "almost makes the stones creep." Meade finally persuaded Birney to bring his division forward, but by then the situation at the front was so bad that he finally had to order a retreat in order to save his command. As Meade and his men fell back across the open field over which they had so successfully advanced just a short time before, the general encountered Reynolds and made no attempt to conceal his exasperation at what had just transpired. "My God," he angrily asked Reynolds, "did they think my division could whip Lee's whole army?"[4]

Meade's breakthrough proved to be the only tactical success the Federal army would achieve at Fredericksburg. With the failure of Franklin's feeble effort, Burnside decided that victory would have to come from Sumner's attacks, and he persisted in ordering a series of bloody and fruitless assaults on Lee's position at Marye's Heights. By the end of the day, it was clear that the Federals had suffered a disaster of horrific magnitude. On December 14 Burnside relented to the pleas of his generals not to launch yet another attack at Fredericksburg and decided to recross the Rappahannock.

To anyone who questioned the efficacy of the overland approach to Richmond, Pope's and Burnside's failures provided plenty of support for their views. "The army are [sic] willing enough to go to Richmond," Meade remarked after Fredericksburg. "Two routes have already been tried this fall—the one by Gordonsville and this by Fredericksburg. Both have failed, and the only one deemed by military men as practicable they obstinately refuse to let us take—by the Peninsula."[5] Lincoln, however, refused to consider a return to the James River line, even after Franklin and Sixth Corps commander Maj. Gen. William F. Smith, disturbed over the fruitless carnage of Fredericksburg, submitted to the president a memorandum containing a well-reasoned and vigorously argued case for such a move.

However frustrating the Fredericksburg Campaign had been for Meade, his performance attracted favorable attention throughout the army. In recognition of this Burnside decided to elevate him to command of the Fifth Corps. Fortunately for Meade, this unit was one of the best in the army. Its first commander, Fitz John Porter, had been one of the most respected junior officers in the regular army before the war, and in 1861 he clearly emerged as McClellan's favorite subordinate. Porter's ability as an organizer and tactician was manifest in the quality of the corps, to which McClellan had consistently assigned tough assignments during the Peninsula Campaign and Seven Days' Battles. The division commanders, Brig. Gens. Andrew A. Humphreys, Charles Griffin, and Maj. Gen. George Sykes, were as good as any commander could hope for.

Yet for all of the unit's admirable qualities, command of the Fifth Corps was far from an ideal assignment. Because of its

DANIEL BUTTERFIELD

Born New York 1831, son of John Butterfield of the Overland Mail Company; graduated from Union College; spent the pre-war years studying law and as superintendent of the eastern division of American Express Company; became colonel of the 12th New York Militia; when war broke out the regiment was accepted into Federal service; on May 24, 1861, it become the first Union regiment to enter the state of Virginia; in September 1861 commissioned a brigadier general of volunteers and given a brigade in George Morrell's division that was later assigned to the V Corps of the Army of the Potomac; fought through the Peninsula campaign, at Gaines Mill he seized a regimental flag to rally his men and was seriously wounded, in 1892 he would be awarded the Medal of Honor for his actions there; returned to duty and served at Second Manassas and Antietam; after which he suc-
ceeded Morrell as division commander; in November 1862 promoted to major general and given command of the V Corps, which he led against the stone wall on Marye's Heights at Fredericksburg; when Hooker replaced Burnside, Butterfield became his chief of staff, performed well and among other things helped to design the corps badges for the Army; continued as chief of staff for Meade, was wounded in the artillery barrage that preceded Pickett's Charge at Gettysburg; after which he became involved in a quarrel with Meade over whether or not he had considered retreating after the second day; transferred to the Army of the Cumberland where he was again Hooker's chief of staff during the Chattanooga campaign; in the Atlanta campaign commanded the 3rd division in Hooker's XX Corps, became too ill to command in July 1864, and did not recover in time to have another field command before the war ended; after the war was active in several business pursuits, veterans organizations, and was a close friend of President Grant, dying on July 17, 1901, at Cold Spring, New York. Butterfield is best known for composing the song "Taps" during the Peninsula campaign.

close association with McClellan and Porter, there were many in Washington who viewed it with suspicion and consequently were highly sensitive regarding its commander. Maj. Gen. Daniel Butterfield's appointment to command the corps in November 1862 had been a source of relief to those politicians, in part because, not having attended the military academy, he was presumed to be free of the influence of the West Point clique associated with McClellan. Certainly the fact that Hooker, a friend of Butterfield, protested the change in command hurt Meade politically and exacerbated the difficult situation in which the new corps commander found himself.

Butterfield, needless to say, was exceedingly displeased at Burnside's decision. Yet despite the fact that Hooker's star was on the rise in Washington, his efforts to reverse the change in command of the Fifth Corps were to no avail. Butterfield and Hooker, however, were not men who forgave or forgot slights. Through no fault of his own, Meade had acquired powerful enemies and become a matter of concern to some in Washington.

Meade had been fortunate up until this time in his relations with the government. To be sure, it was not difficult for anyone sensitive to such things to figure out where a West Point–trained officer who preferred to associate with members of the McClellan clique probably stood on the various points of conflict between Washington and the Army of the Potomac. Yet as a brigade and division commander, Meade had not been in a position prominent enough to have much contact with politicians or attract the sort of political scrutiny that other officers had during the first year of the war. And unlike some of his fellow officers, he was smart enough to refrain from conspicuous public expressions of his deepening discontent with Washington's management of military affairs, having instead confined his complaints to private letters to his wife. Moreover, beginning the war as a brigade commander had given Meade the opportunity to establish a reputation as a fighting general and first-rate combat leader. His consistently excellent performances on the battlefield certainly made it difficult for anyone by the end of 1862 to deny that he had earned his elevation to corps command.

Meade's first operation as commander of the Fifth Corps was the disastrous "Mud March" of January 20–23, 1863. Recognizing that defeat at Fredericksburg had not diminished the administration's desire that something be done to get at the Rebels along the Rappahannock line, Burnside decided to try to turn Lee's strong position by marching along the north bank of the Rappahannock and crossing several miles above the Confederate left. Unfortunately, at the end of the first day of the flanking march, the heavens opened up and turned the roads into streams of mud. Burnside persisted in the march, but on January 23 he finally conceded defeat. The Army of the Potomac then marched back to its camp at Falmouth and established winter quarters.

Although unhappy at the situation, Meade personally went to Burnside and expressed sympathy for his plight. ("I never felt so disappointed and sorry for any one in my life as I did for Burnside," Meade told his wife after meeting with the general. "He really seems to have even the elements against him.")[6] Burnside was appreciative and confided to Meade that he was contemplating major changes in the army's high command. Ever since the Fredericksburg debacle, a steady stream of officers, including Franklin and Hooker, had been complaining to Washington about Burnside's leadership and reporting that his failures were fostering a spirit of rapidly spreading discontent within the army. Burnside, naturally, sought to counter the growing crisis by getting rid of such troublesome men. If his plans were approved, Burnside informed Meade that he would take Hooker's place as commander of one of the grand divisions.

When Burnside advised Washington of his plans to cashier the disgruntled generals, he let it be known in no uncertain terms that if the dismissals were not accepted, he would resign his commission. Although appreciative of the general's willingness to deflect criticism of the administration by publicly accepting full responsibility for the Fredericksburg disaster, Lincoln refused to fully accept Burnside's plan to recast the army's high command. Yet he also recognized that Burnside could no longer remain as commander of the Army of the Potomac. Consequently, on January 26 Lincoln appointed Joseph Hooker to replace Burnside as army commander and, instead of accepting the general's resignation, sent him out west to take command in Ohio. Immediately after assuming the command he had long sought, Hooker abolished the grand-division organizational plan, and Meade remained in command of the Fifth Corps.

Although unable to completely set aside his concerns about the new army commander's boastfulness, poor selection of associates, and general low character, Meade decided to give "Fighting Joe" the benefit of the doubt as he took command of the army. "I believe Hooker is a good soldier," he told his wife, "the danger he runs is of subjecting himself to bad influences, such as Dan Butterfield and Dan Sickles. . . . I believe my opinion is more favorable than any other of the old regular officers, most of whom are decided in their hostility to him."[7]

When the results of Hooker's extraordinary efforts to rebuild the army became manifest, Meade was delighted. Hooker had worked wonders. By late April 1863, a combination of better food, regular pay, diligent training, and liberal furlough policies had completely restored the army's spirits and health, both of which had been badly damaged by the Fredericksburg debacle and the Mud March.

Hooker proved equally adept at operational planning. He conceived a plan, similar to the one Burnside had attempted to implement in January, whereby a portion of the army would cross the Rappahannock and threaten the Confederate position at Fredericksburg. While Lee was busy dealing with this force, the bulk of the Army of the Potomac would move west along the left bank of the Rappahannock, then cross it and the Rapidan River. This would turn the Confederate left and force Lee to either retreat south from Fredericksburg or risk being trapped between the two wings of the Federal army.

On April 27 Hooker roused his army from their camps and began the movement upriver. The Eleventh and Twelfth Corps led the march, followed by Meade's Fifth Corps. Two days later Meade's command crossed the Rappahannock and Rapidan

Rivers and moved into a thickly forested area known as the Wilderness. The Wilderness was a terrible place for the Union army to operate. Only a few easily obstructed roads passed through the area, which effectively neutralized its overwhelming superiority in manpower and artillery. Fortunately, once the army was east of the crossroads near the Chancellor House, known as Chancellorsville, it would again be in the open and able to take advantage of its superior firepower and numbers.

By late afternoon on April 30, four powerful Federal corps had reached the Chancellorsville crossroads. Lee's army was still at Fredericksburg, preparing to deal with the Federals who had crossed the river there. Meade could not contain his excitement. When Maj. Gen. Henry Slocum, commander of the Twelfth Corps, arrived at Chancellorsville, Meade exclaimed: "This is splendid. . . . Hurrah for old Joe; we are on Lee's flank, and he does not know it. You take the Plank Road toward Fredericksburg, and I'll take the Pike, or vice versa, as you prefer, and we'll get out of this Wilderness."[8]

Hooker arrived at Chancellorsville a few hours later and decided that his army would not continue any farther east that day, even though there was still plenty of daylight left. Hooker nonetheless was even more sanguine than Meade in his assessment of the situation. "Operations of the last three days," he had already informed the army in a congratulatory order, "have determined that the enemy must either ingloriously fly, or come out from behind his defenses and give us battle on our own ground, where certain destruction awaits him." To make his victory secure, Hooker ordered yet another corps, the Third, commanded by his favorite subordinate, Maj. Gen. Dan Sickles, to move to Chancellorsville. His confidence soared. "The rebel army," Hooker proclaimed, "is now the legitimate property of the Army of the Potomac. . . . God Almighty could not prevent [our] destroying the rebel army."[9]

Although the Third Corps was quickly moving toward Chancellorsville, Hooker decided not to await its arrival to begin his march on May 1. He directed Meade to lead Humphreys's and Griffin's divisions east along the River Road toward Banks' Ford and send his other division, under Sykes,

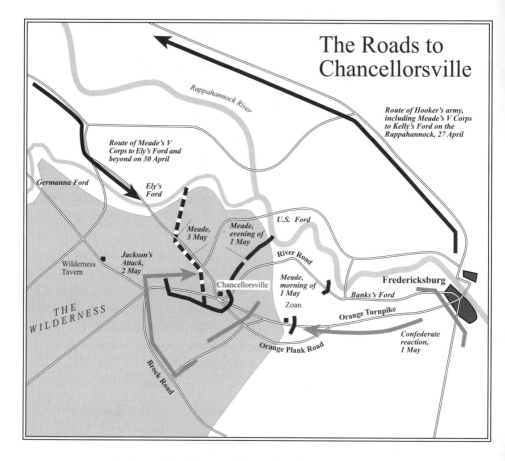

The Roads to Chancellorsville

Rappahannock River

Route of Hooker's army, including Meade's V Corps to Kelly's Ford on the Rappahannock, 27 April

Route of Meade's V Corps to Ely's Ford and beyond on 30 April

Germanna Ford

Ely's Ford

Meade, 3 May

Meade, evening of 1 May

U.S. Ford

Jackson's Attack, 2 May

Wilderness Tavern

River Road

Chancellorsville

Meade, morning of 1 May

Fredericksburg

Banks's Ford

Zoan

THE WILDERNESS

Orange Turnpike

Confederate reaction, 1 May

Orange Plank Road

Brock Road

east along the Orange Turnpike. Slocum's corps would move along the Orange Plank Road farther south. If all went according to plan, Meade's and Slocum's advances would lead the army out of the Wilderness and establish a line from which a decisive push against Lee's army could be made.

Meade encountered little resistance as he led Humphreys's and Griffin's divisions east along the River Road, and within a few hours, the column's lead elements had reached high ground "within view of Banks' Ford, without any opposition from the enemy."[10] Meade was delighted. If his men could secure control of the ford, it would greatly ease Hooker's efforts to coordinate the two wings of the army.

CHARLES GRIFFIN

Born Ohio 1825; graduated U.S. Military Academy 1847, twenty-third out of a class of thirty-eight; brevetted 2d Lieutenant in the artillery; sent to Mexico but arrived after most of the fighting was over; served at various frontier posts until 1860, when he became an instructor at West Point in artillery tactics; in 1861 organized a field battery from the artillerymen stationed at West Point, Griffin became its captain and led the "West Point battery" with distinction at First Manassas; his service there led to his promotion to major; during the Peninsula Campaign was commissioned brigadier general of volunteers and given command of a brigade in General Fitz John Porter's V Corps; was involved in the quarrel between Porter and General John Pope after Second Manassas that led to Porter's removal from command, Griffin retained his command despite his stanch defense of Porter; held in reserve at Antietam; given command of the 1st division of the V Corps, which he led a futile assault against Marye's Heights at Fredericksburg; saw limited action at Chancellorsville and missed most of the Gettysburg Campaign due to illness; led his division through the Wilderness, Spotsylvania,  Cold Harbor, and finally to Petersburg; always unable to hide his displeasure, one especially vehement harangue against his superiors during the Battle of the Wilderness led Grant to recommend his arrest; Meade successfully brushed aside the suggestion by saying that it was simply Griffin's way; at Five Forks he was placed in command of the V Corps after Sheridan removed Warren; the next day he was promoted to major general of volunteers; at Appomattox he was appointed one of the commissioners to carry out the surrender terms; after the war Griffin was stationed in the District of Texas and refused to leave Galveston during a yellow fever outbreak; he died of the disease on September 15, 1867 and is buried in Georgetown, DC.

To the south, however, Sykes's and Slocum's advances encountered stiff Confederate resistance when they reached a ridge near Zoan Church. Thanks to the efforts of his cavalry, Lee had found out about Hooker's move to Chancellorsville. To deal with the Federal army bearing down on his rear, Lee daringly decided to divide his forces, leaving a small force at Fredericksburg to confront Maj. Gen. John Sedgwick, while he led the bulk of his command toward Chancellorsville.

DANIEL E. SICKLES

Born New York City 1825; attended New York City University to study law; admitted to the bar in 1843; after discovering politics to be a more promising field, became a Democrat in New York City's infamous Tammany Hall political machine; in 1847 he was elected to the New York State Assembly, where he helped obtain support for the creation of Central Park in New York City, he was also censored for escorting a known prostitute into the legislative chambers; in 1853 appointed secretary to James Buchanan, who was then minister to England. Sickles created another scandal by taking this same prostitute with him and introducing her to Queen Victoria, giving her the surname of a political rival; elected to the New York State Senate in 1855; served in the U.S. House of Representatives from 1857-1861. In 1859 Sickles achieved national notoriety for murdering the son of Francis Scott Key for having an affair with his wife, at a sensational trial, Sickles's defense attorney, Edwin M. Stanton, who served as secretary of war during the Civil War, won his acquittal by reason of temporary insanity; this was the first successful use of the defense in the U.S. At the outbreak of the war Sickles used his political connections to gain commission as a brigadier general of volunteers and command of the 'Excelsior Brigade' in Joseph Hooker's division of the Third Corps, which he had been involved in recruiting; participated in the battles of Seven Pines and the Seven Days; in September 1862 given command of a division and in

Unfortunately for the Federals, Lee's bold decision and Sykes's and Slocum's encounter with the Confederates unnerved Hooker. He immediately issued orders directing Meade and Slocum to fall back from the Zoan Church ridge into the Wilderness and take up a line around Chancellorsville. Meade was incredulous at this abrupt reversal. "My God," he remarked as he pulled his men back, "if we can't hold the top of a hill, we certainly can't hold the bottom of it!" That after-

November promoted to major general; after Fredericksburg promoted to command of the III Corps; at Chancellorsville elements of his corps detected Stonewall Jackson's flank march and attacked its rear guard, the next day his command was ordered to abandon the key position of Hazel Grove, which the Confederates subsequently used for massed artillery fire into his troops; already on bad terms with Meade, on the second day of the Battle of Gettysburg Sickles ignored his commander's orders and redeployed his corps on his own initiative in a new position far in advance of the rest of the Union line; there it was quickly overrun by a massive Confederate assault; Sickles was severely wounded by a Confederate cannon ball and would endure the amputation of his right leg; the day after his surgery Sickles left for Washington to present his case to Lincoln before Meade could; thus began a lifelong controversy with Meade over the battle that badly hurt both Sickles's and Meade's reputations; after his petition to return to field command was rejected by Meade, Sickles's next important service was as a member of a fact-finding mission for President Lincoln on the progress of Reconstruction in Union occupied areas of the South; after the war he became a diplomat, serving as U.S. Minister to Spain, where he reportedly conducted an affair with Queen Isabella II; in 1886 appointed chairman of the New York state monument commission, which he would be removed from in 1912 for mishandling funds; in 1893 he returned to Congress where he helped create Gettysburg National Military Park; described in his old age as "old, irresponsible and cantankerous," he died at age ninety-four in 1914 and was buried in Arlington National Cemetery. His amputated leg, however, is preserved at the Armed Forces Medical Museum in Washington, where he would visit it before he died; it is still on display there today. Always controversial, Sickles remains one of the most fascinating characters in American history.

noon, Second Corps commander Maj. Gen. Darius Couch came away from a conversation with Hooker convinced "that my commanding general was a whipped man." One staff officer wrote: "Hooker was at a loss to know what to do. He seemed to me to be completely dumbfounded."[11]

After falling back along the Banks' Ford road, Meade's corps went into position on the Federal left, facing east, with Couch's corps on its right and the Rappahannock River on its left. By the morning of May 2, Hooker had established a formidable line facing east and south from Chancellorsville. To Couch's right rested Slocum's corps, with Sickles's Third Corps next to it, holding an excellent piece of terrain known as Hazel Grove. Finally, Maj. Gen. Oliver O. Howard's Eleventh Corps stood in reserve to the west of Chancellorsville along the Orange Turnpike.

Although vastly outnumbered, Lee decided to attack Hooker. After learning on May 1 from his cavalry that the Federal right was vulnerable, he boldly decided to send Stonewall Jackson's corps on a long march around the Federal flank. Jackson began his march early on the morning of May 2, and by the afternoon he was deploying astride the Orange Turnpike just west of Howard's position. Although Hooker warned Howard to keep a watch out in that direction after receiving reports of Jackson's march, the Eleventh Corps was caught completely off guard when the Confederates attacked. By 6:00 P.M., Howard's corps was in full retreat toward Chancellorsville.

Hooker quickly began redeploying his army to deal with the crisis. Aided by darkness, he was able to establish a new line less than a half mile from Chancellorsville and frustrate Jackson's efforts to sustain the momentum of his attack. At Hooker's direction Meade promptly shifted his corps westward and formed a line along Ely's Ford Road to protect the army's line of retreat to the only crossing of the Rappahannock in its rear, U.S. Ford, and cover Howard's shattered command as it attempted to reform.

Meade hoped to do more. On the morning of May 3, a staff officer suggested to the general that the Confederates west of

Chancellorsville, now commanded by Maj. Gen. J.E.B. Stuart after Jackson was wounded the previous evening, might be vulnerable to a strong counterattack from his position. With Reynolds's First Corps arriving on the battlefield and its commander eager to pitch in, Meade agreed with the assessment and decided to go to army headquarters at the Chancellor House. He found Hooker, but the army commander was in bad shape after being stunned by a pillar that was knocked over by a Confederate shell. Hooker possessed enough energy, however, to promptly throw cold water on Meade's proposal. A furious Meade returned to his corps's position along Ely Ford Road, where he spent the rest of the day listening impotently as, just to the south, Stuart launched a series of furious assaults across his front against the Union line west of Chancellorsville.

That night, Meade made one more plea for a counterattack to envelop Stuart's left during a council of war Hooker convened at his headquarters. He quickly found out, however, that Hooker had come to the meeting with his mind already fixed on retreat, with Sickles supporting that view. "As a soldier," one staff officer wrote, "[Sickles] advised him not to fall back, but as Washington was in danger as a politician he advised him to fall back." Meade was dumbfounded by this logic. He immediately responded to Sickles's remark by stating, "if those were the motives which influenced this army, he did not see why we had crossed the river at all" and argued vehemently against retreat. Every other officer at the meeting agreed with Meade that the army should stay and fight. Hooker and Sickles, however, had made up their minds—the army would recross the Rappahannock. "What was the use of calling us together at this time of night," Reynolds asked Couch afterward, "when he intended to retreat anyhow?"[12] With Meade's corps covering the retreat, Hooker pulled his army back across the Rappahannock the next day.

In the aftermath of the Chancellorsville fiasco, all confidence the Army of the Potomac's high command had in Hooker evaporated. Talk of his replacement began among the corps commanders almost the moment the army had returned to its camps north of the Rappahannock. Meade's efforts to steel Hooker's backbone during the battle had particularly impressed his fellow generals, and many of them concluded that he was the man to lead the army. When some attempted to secure Meade's support for a petition urging Hooker's removal, however, he sharply rebuked them. He also maintained his practice of not publicly expressing his discontent with the state of affairs, even when Lincoln and Halleck called him in for a closed-door meeting. In his private letters, however, Meade advised his wife: "Hooker has disappointed the army and myself in failing to show the nerve . . . at the critical moment, which all had given him credit for before he was tried. . . . I am sorry for Hooker, because I like him and my relations have always been agreeable with him; but I cannot shut my eyes to the fact that he has on this occasion missed a brilliant opportunity."[13]

Meade's unwillingness to be more open in his criticism was no doubt motivated in part by his desire not to encourage the growing movement for placing him in command of the army. In response to a letter from his wife, who lamented that such a move "would only be your ruin," Meade was unequivocal. "The command of this army," he advised her, "is not to be desired or sought for . . . ; it is more likely to destroy one's reputation than to add to it."[14]

Hooker evidently did not agree, and after the battle ended, he began a successful campaign to reassure his backers in Congress. Lincoln, of course, was well aware of Fighting Joe's political standing and decided to keep him in command. If only because it kept him out of a post that he desired to avoid, Meade was more amenable than most of the army's corps commanders to Hooker's retention in command.

The opportunity to redeem himself came quickly to Hooker. After Chancellorsville, Lee decided to embark on another offensive across the Potomac. When Lincoln rejected a plan to take advantage of Lee's move by attacking Richmond, Hooker turned his army around and began moving north in an effort to counter his opponent's movements. Although he fulfilled the administration's mandate of keeping the Army of the Potomac between Lee and Washington, the tone of Hooker's messages and his refusal to take his corps commanders into his confidence regarding his plans exacerbated the concerns of superiors and subordinates alike. "This is what Joe Hooker thinks profound sagacity," an exasperated Meade wrote his wife, "keeping his corps commanders, who are to execute his plans, in total ignorance."[15]

Meade's despair over Hooker was shared by Lincoln, who finally decided on June 27 that a change in command was necessary. By then, Meade was more than ready to see Fighting Joe depart, in part because he was sure that if Lincoln removed Hooker, politics would so influence the choice of his successor that there was little chance the burden of army command would fall upon his own shoulders. "I have no friends, political or others, who press or advance my claims or pretensions," he assured his wife, "and there are so many others who are pressed by influential politicians that it is folly to think I stand any chance upon mere merit alone."[16] On June 28 the general's optimism would be rudely shattered.

4
GETTYSBURG COMMANDER

Lee's second crossing of the Potomac River was a response to the fact that, despite his brilliant victory at Chancellorsville, the Confederacy faced serious problems as spring turned to summer in 1863. Out west, Union general Ulysses S. Grant had finally figured out a solution to the problem of Vicksburg, the capture of which would complete the Union effort to regain control of the Mississippi River. Moreover, war weariness was on the rise in the South, supplies of all resources were dwindling rapidly, and there seemed to be no end to the resources available to Northern forces, which were growing stronger every day. Neither a passive defensive along the Rappahannock nor the dispatch of troops from the Army of Northern Virginia to Mississippi, as some within the Confederate government were pushing for, would solve any of these problems. The only possible way for the Confederacy to place itself on the road to victory, Lee managed to persuade his political masters, was to take the offensive and win a battle on Northern soil so convincing that it would break the enemy's will to continue the fight.

Although Lee's move north provoked great consternation in the Northern press, it delighted President Lincoln. The Second Manassas, Fredericksburg, and Chancellorsville debacles had provided such vivid illustrations of the operational and tactical problems associated with the overland route that by May 1863, Lincoln had accepted stalemate in Virginia as the price to be paid for keeping the Army of the Potomac between Washington and the enemy. Lee's crossing the Potomac, however, completely transformed the operational situation and created an opportunity for the Union army to fight the Army of Northern Virginia far from its base, outside of its strong positions behind the Rappahannock and Rapidan Rivers, and strike it a crippling blow. "We cannot help beating them," Lincoln exulted in a conversation with a member of his cabinet, "if we have the man." Tempering his optimism, however, was the question of whether Hooker would "commit the same fault as McClellan [during the 1862 Maryland Campaign] and lose his chance." Did Fighting Joe Hooker possess the ability and energy to seize what the president considered "the best opportunity [for a decisive victory in the East] we have had since the war began"?[1] On June 27 Lincoln decided once and for all that the answer was "no."

Despite his own discontent with Hooker, as the Federal army moved north toward the Potomac River in pursuit of Lee's army, Meade continued to provide vigorous leadership to the Fifth Corps. On June 27 he pushed his command across the Potomac at Edwards Ferry and marched it to a point just south of Frederick, Maryland. After his men settled in to their new camp, Meade rode off in search of Hooker or anyone else who might be able to confirm rumors as to the location of Lee's army or even the rest of the Army of the Potomac.

As Meade undertook what would prove to be a fruitless search, he was unaware that a momentous decision had been made earlier that day in Washington. Hooker, after a bitter dispute with Henry Halleck over the garrison at Harpers Ferry, had submitted his resignation. Lincoln, to the general's surprise, immediately accepted it and decided to appoint Meade as his successor. The task of informing Meade of the change and telling him that "the order for him to assume command of the army immediately was intended to be as unquestionable and peremptory as any that a soldier could receive" was entrusted to Col. James Hardie. Late in the evening of June 27, Hardie boarded a train bound for Frederick.[2]

It took the colonel nearly three hours after his arrival at Frederick to find Meade, who had returned to his headquarters after failing to locate Hooker, and present him with orders placing him in command of the Army of the Potomac as well as instructions from Halleck. Meade learned that he was expected to "maneuver and fight in such a manner as to cover the capital and also Baltimore. . . . Should General Lee move upon either of these places, it is expected that you will either anticipate him or arrive with him so as to give him battle." As long as he kept in mind "the important fact that the Army of the Potomac is the covering army of Washington," Halleck assured Meade that he was "free to act as you may deem proper" and would not be "hampered by any minute instructions from these headquarters." To further impress upon Meade the gravity of the situation and that "no one ever received a more important command," Halleck also took the extraordinary step of giving him the authority to dismiss any subordinate officer and ignore seniority when assigning command responsibilities.[3]

After his meeting with Hardie, Meade called on Brig. Gen. Gouverneur Warren and offered him the post of army chief of staff. Warren declined, however, on the grounds that, although chief engineer of the army, he did not know enough about the rest of the army to fill the job of chief of staff adequately in the present crisis. Thus, Meade reluctantly decided to retain Maj. Gen. Daniel Butterfield as chief of staff until the military situation was more settled. After talking with Warren, Meade located Hardie shortly before dawn, and together the two men rode off to find Hooker and deliver the orders relieving him from command. After reaching Hooker's headquarters and informing him of the change of command, Meade summoned Butterfield.

When the chief of staff arrived, Meade and Hooker held an impromptu council of war in which the latter described the current dispositions of the army's various corps. What

Hooker's plans were Meade was unable to discern, and he "unguardedly expressed himself," one observer later recalled, "shocked at the scattered condition of the army," but the meeting did provide him with some sense of what he had to work with. After the meeting ended at 7:00 A.M., Meade sent a message to Washington stating: "The order placing me in command of this army is received. As a soldier I obey it. . . . I can only say now that it appears to me I must move toward the Susquehanna, keeping Washington and Baltimore well covered, and if the enemy is checked in his attempt to cross the Susquehanna or if he turns toward Baltimore, to give him battle." Halleck wrote back: "I fully concur in your general views as to the movements of your army. All available assistance will be given to you."[4]

The president, his hopes so often dashed by generals, hoped that, though reported to be a general of the McClellan stripe, Meade, as a Pennsylvanian at least, would "fight well on his own dunghill." Although there were many who had thought the emergency would compel the Lincoln administration to restore McClellan to command, Meade's appointment met with acceptance, if not enthusiasm, within the Army of the Potomac. One postwar writer recalled that Meade, although not "what is called a popular officer, . . . was much respected by his comrades in arms. He was known in the army as one who had grown up with it, whose advancement was due to merit, and who had shown a special steadfastness in many trying hours." Artillerist Charles Wainwright spoke for many in the army's high command when he commented, "Meade was my candidate for Hooker's successor . . . , believing him to have the longest and clearest head of any general officer in this army." For his part, Lee immediately recognized that a general such as Meade, cut from the same cloth as McClellan, was not, as were Hooker and Pope, to be taken lightly. "Meade," he warily predicted, "will commit no blunder in my front, and if I make one he will make haste to take advantage."[5]

Meade's first step, after meeting with Hooker and Butterfield, was to find someone he could trust to discuss the situation with and make sure he had his army well in hand. Thus, he was particularly pleased when First Corps commander John Reynolds suddenly appeared at headquarters to express his satisfaction at the change of command and find out what Meade planned to do. Although formerly his superior, Reynolds was immensely relieved and gratified at Meade's elevation to army command. It eliminated the despised Hooker from the picture in favor of a fellow McClellanite. Plus it meant that Reynolds, who previously had been sounded out on the position—and in no uncertain terms let it be known he would not accept command unless he was granted complete autonomy from Washington strategists— had once again managed to evade what he, like Meade, considered an extremely undesirable position.

JOHN F. REYNOLDS

Born Lancaster, Pennsylvania 1820 (some 50 miles from the place of his greatest glory and death, Gettysburg); graduated U.S. Military Academy 1841, twenty-sixth in a class of fifty-two; brevetted 2d lieutenant in the 3rd Artillery, served garrison duty mainly in the South; 1st Lieutenant 1846; ordered to join Zachary Taylor's army in Texas, During the Mexican War, participated in the defense of Fort Texas (later renamed Fort Brown), brevetted to captain for service at the battle of Monterrey, at Buena Vista his section of guns prevented a flanking movement by the Mexican cavalry and helped repulse the final Mexican charge, cited for gallantry after the battle and brevetted to major; accompanied Colonel Albert Sidney Johnston's expedition during the Mormon Rebellion, appointed commandant of cadets at West Point in September 1860, where he was when war broke out in 1861; appointed brigadier general of volunteers in August 1861 and given command of a brigade in the "Pennsylvania Reserves" division, his brigade stood fast at Mechanicsville, at Gaines Mill the next day he

The new commander decided to abandon Hooker's vaguely developed plan to operate in the Shenandoah Valley against Lee's communications. Instead, Meade told Reynolds to take his corps and advance north in the direction of a Pennsylvania crossroads town named Gettysburg in search of the enemy. The rest of the Army of the Potomac, meanwhile, would concentrate at Frederick and then move north and east in the direction of York, Pennsylvania. On Parr's Ridge overlooking Pipe Creek, the army could establish a strong defensive position that would cover the roads that led from Pennsylvania to Baltimore and provide a secure base from which it could conduct offensive operations to relieve Harrisburg if, as reports suggested, the Pennsylvania state capital was Lee's objective.

led a rear guard action that covered Porter's retreat, but in the chaos was cut off from his unit and captured; confined in Libby Prison until his exchange for William Barksdale in August 1862; given command of the Pennsylvania Reserves division, he led it successfully in the Second Manassas campaign; during the Maryland Campaign appointed commander of Pennsylvania Militia and thus missed Antietam; returned to the Army of the Potomac as a major general and given command of the I Corps; at Fredericksburg his assault led by Meade's division on Stonewall Jackson's line was the only breakthrough the Union achieved, but was pushed back by Confederate reinforcements; at Chancellorsville his corps was unengaged; after the battle offered command of the Army of the Potomac by President Lincoln, he refused unless given complete independence from Washington, Lincoln gave command to his former subordinate Meade instead; accepting his new superior without complaint, he was given command of the Left Wing of the Army of the Potomac (the I, III, and XI Corps); on July 1, 1863, he made the decision to stand and fight at Gettysburg, while leading the advance of the 2d Wisconsin on McPherson's Ridge against a Confederate position he was killed, and buried at Lancaster on July 4, 1863. Lt. Frank Haskell, an aide to General John Gibbon, wrote about Reynolds death by saying "His death at this time affected us very much, for he was one of the *soldier* Generals of the army, a man whose soul was in his country's work, which he did with a soldier's high honor and fidelity."

With his army well in hand around Frederick by the evening of June 28, Meade began implementing the second part of his plan the following morning. Reynolds's First and Oliver Howard's Eleventh Corps would march toward Emmitsburg under Reynolds's overall command, while the rest of the army marched to Pipe Creek. "If Lee is moving for Baltimore," he informed Halleck, "I expect to get between his main army and that place. If he is crossing the Susquehanna, I shall rely on General Couch [commander of Pennsylvania state militia], with his force holding him there until I can fall upon his rear and give him battle. . . . My endeavor will be in my movements to hold my force well together, with the hope of falling upon some portion of Lee's army in detail."[6]

On June 29 the army advanced twenty miles north from Frederick on what turned out to be a brutally hot and humid day. That day Meade moved his headquarters to Middleburg, Maryland, and informed Halleck that all reports indicated that Lee's entire army was in Pennsylvania. "The enemy are on our soil," Meade informed his army the next day. "Homes, firesides, and domestic altars are involved. The army has fought well heretofore; it is believed that it will fight more desperately and bravely than ever. . . . Corps and other commanders are authorized to order the instant death of any soldier who fails in his duty at this hour."[7]

Meade, however, planned to make only a short march on June 30 that would carry all but the First and Eleventh Corps north and east in the direction of York, Pennsylvania, where Confederate infantry was reported to be in force. But around noon Meade received a report indicating that Lee was pulling back his advanced corps from York and Carlisle and was probably looking to concentrate his forces "at or near Chambersburg." Meade responded by directing Dan Sickles to move his corps north and west toward Emmitsburg to reinforce the two corps already there under Reynolds that were scheduled to advance to Gettysburg on July 1. Upon reaching Taneytown and establishing his headquarters, Meade also directed Warren and artillerist Henry J. Hunt to thoroughly survey a fallback position on the high ground overlooking Pipe

Creek. "All is going well," Meade informed his wife at the end of the day. "I have relieved Harrisburg and Philadelphia. . . . I continue well, but much oppressed with a sense of responsibility and the magnitude of the great interests entrusted me."[8]

Warren and Hunt did their work exceedingly well and traced out a position between Middleburg and Manchester that effectively covered the roads leading to Baltimore and the new Union supply base at Westminster, Maryland. With this in hand and further evidence arriving that Lee had withdrawn his advanced units west from York and Carlisle, at noon on July 1 Meade reported to Halleck: "my advance has answered its purpose. I shall not advance any, but prepare to receive an attack in case Lee makes one. . . . [H]aving relieved the pressure on the Susquehanna, I am now looking to the protection of Washington and fighting my army to the best advantage."[9]

Meade then issued a circular to his army laying out his intentions for July 1. If the Rebels attacked, the general expected to hold them in check, then "withdraw the army from its present position, and form line of battle with the left resting in the neighborhood of Middleburg, and the right at Manchester, the general direction being that of Pipe Creek." Once there, John Sedgwick's corps would form the right of the army near Manchester, while the Fifth and Twelfth Corps under the overall command of Maj. Gen. Henry Slocum would hold the center near Union Mills. After withdrawing from Gettysburg and Emmitsburg, the First, Eleventh, and Third Corps, under Reynolds's direction, would fall back to the vicinity of Middleburg to hold the Union left. Maj. Gen. Winfield Scott Hancock's Second Corps would be posted at Uniontown to form the reserve.[10]

Once in position behind Pipe Creek, the Army of the Potomac would present Lee with an incredibly difficult, if not impossible, operational and tactical problem. The defensive position effectively covered all of the roads leading to Baltimore and Washington and, with the railhead at Westminster immediately to its rear, provided the Union army with secure logistics. Moreover, the skill with which Warren and Hunt laid out the Federal line, combined with the terrain and Union superiority in artillery and engineering, provided Meade with unassailable flanks and an engagement area to his front that would make a Confederate frontal assault suicidal. In addition, a Union army positioned behind Pipe Creek would be on the flank of Lee's line of communications running through the Shenandoah Valley. This would make any Confederate position in Pennsylvania untenable and put the Army of the Potomac in a perfect position from which it could fall upon Lee's flank when he retreated back to Virginia. Hunt would later recall with justifiable pride: "all of the elements of the problem [Meade faced] were in favor of the Pipe Creek line. . . . It probably would have been better had he concentrated his army behind Pipe Creek rather than Gettysburg." To Hunt's regret, though, "July 1st changed the situation."[11]

Before dawn that day, a message reached Meade reporting that Brig. Gen. John Buford, commander of the cavalry forces screening Reynolds's wing of the army, had spotted a large body of Confederate infantry near Gettysburg the previous day. Secure in the knowledge that Reynolds was near the scene with the First and Eleventh Corps and would soon be occupying Gettysburg, Meade decided not to make any major changes in the deployment of his army preparatory to a withdrawal to Pipe Creek but instead to await events.

Shortly before noon, Capt. Stephen Weld of Reynolds's staff arrived at Meade's headquarters and informed the army commander that Buford's cavalry and the First Corps were engaged with a large Confederate force west of Gettysburg. Reynolds, Weld reported, was determined to hold off the Rebels in order to deny them the use of the superb terrain south of the town. To this end, Reynolds had vowed to "fight them inch by inch, and, if driven into the town, I will barricade the streets and hold them back as long as possible." "Good!" Meade replied, "That is just like Reynolds; he will hold on to the bitter end."[12] Secure that his friend could handle whatever Lee might throw at him until reinforcements arrived, Meade began reorienting the rest of his army's movements so it could respond to what was taking place at Gettysburg.

The Gettysburg Campaign
June–July 1863

THIRTY MILES

Harrisburg

EWELL

Carlisle

York

Chambersburg

Gettysburg

LONGSTREET
HILL

Hanover

MEADE

Emmitsburg

Manchester

Hagerstown

Union Mills

Williamsport

REYNOLDS

Middleburg

Westminister

HOWARD

Uniontown

HANCOCK

Sharpsburg

SICKLES

SYKES

Martinsburg

SLOCUM

SEDGWICK

LEE

Harpers Ferry

Frederick

Baltimore

Winchester

Leesburg

Potomac River

SHENANDOAH VALLEY

HOOKER

ASHBYS GAP

STUART

Washington

Shenandoah River

CHESTER GAP

Alexandria

Manassas Junction

Warrenton Junction

Rappahannock Station

ORANGE & ALEXANDRIA R.R.

Brandy Station

Culpeper C.H.

Aquia Landing

Rapidan River

Fredericksburg

Orange C.H.

Gordonsville

WINFIELD SCOTT HANCOCK

Born Pennsylvania 1824; attended Norristown Academy; graduated from U.S. Military Academy eighteenth in the class of 1844; brevet 2d lieutenant 6th Infantry 1844; 2d lieutenant 1846; participated in Mexican War; brevetted 1st lieutenant 1847 for gallant conduct in the battles of Contreras and Churubusco; following the Mexican War, he spent years as regimental quartermaster and adjutant in Florida, Kansas, Utah, and on the Pacific coast; in 1850 married Almira Russell, daughter of a St. Louis merchant. Promoted to 1st lieutenant 1853; captain in 1855. Appointed brigadier general of volunteers in 1861; prominent in Peninsular Campaign; commanded a division at Antietam; major general volunteers 1862 to 1866; participated in battles of Fredericksburg and Chancellorsville; commanded the Second Corps at Gettysburg, where he achieved lasting fame and the thanks of Congress for turning back the Confederates from the Federal left and center. Hancock never fully recovered from the wound he received at Gettysburg, but commanded his corps in battles from the Wilderness to Petersburg; appointed brigadier general U.S. Army in 1864 for distinguished services; brevetted major general in 1865 for gallant conduct at Spotsylvania. Promoted to major general U.S. Army in 1866; led expedition against hostile Indians in 1867 while commanding the Central Military Department; commanded the Department of Louisiana and Texas in 1867 until Congress removed him for giving civil authorities jurisdiction over all crimes not involving forcible resistance to Federal authority; commanded the Department of Dakota from 1870 to 1872, the Division of the Atlantic from 1872 to 1876, and finally the Department of the East from 1877 to 1886; presidential candidate of the Democratic party in 1880; died at Governors Island, New York, in 1886. A biographer emphasized Hancock's "great industry, courage, ambition, lofty ideals, [and] unfaltering loyalty to friends." General Grant, noting that Hancock never "committed in battle a blunder," praised his "personal courage" and called him "the most conspicuous figure of all the general officers who did not exercise a separate command."

Meade's disposition changed at around 1:00 P.M. when news arrived of Reynolds's death at Gettysburg. Stunned at the loss of his friend and most trusted subordinate, Meade pressed the courier who brought the message for details regarding the situation in Gettysburg. He learned that the First Corps west of Gettysburg and the Eleventh Corps, which upon its arrival on the field had deployed north of the town, were hard pressed. Meade responded by sending Second Corps commander Winfield Scott Hancock to Gettysburg to take charge of the situation. Hancock, in collaboration with Warren, one of the architects of the Pipe Creek line, was also to determine whether the "position there [is] a better one to fight a battle under existing circumstances."[13]

Hancock arrived at Gettysburg around 4:00 P.M. and was greeted with the sight of thousands of Federal soldiers retreating through the town in search of the high ground to the south on Cemetery Hill and Culp's Hill. The combined weight of Lt. Gen. A.P. Hill's attacks from the west and Lt. Gen. Richard Ewell's from the north had completely shattered the initial Federal positions. Hancock and Eleventh Corps commander Howard immediately went to work establishing a strong line on Cemetery Hill and Culp's Hill and, aided by disorganization in the Rebel forces as they attempted to pursue the Northerners through Gettysburg's narrow streets, managed to stabilize the situation by 6:00 P.M. The arrival of part of the Twelfth and Third Corps shortly thereafter further strengthened the Federal position. Hancock sent a message to Meade stating that he could retain his position south of Gettysburg and recommended that the rest of the army be brought up. Confident of Hancock's judgment, Meade cast aside the plan to concentrate at Pipe Creek and ordered the entire army to Gettysburg.

At around 10:00 P.M., Meade left Taneytown, accompanied by his staff and arrived on Cemetery Hill around midnight. Following a brief conversation with Howard in which that officer confirmed Hancock's view that they had a good place to fight, Meade conducted a personal reconnaissance of the area, accompanied by his son Capt. George Meade, Warren, and Hunt. Afterward, Meade retired to the home of a widow Lydia Leister on Cemetery Ridge where he had established his headquarters and began pouring over maps. Although secure in his decision to move the army to Gettysburg, Meade nonetheless also took the prudent step of asking Butterfield to draw up plans should a withdrawal back to the Pipe Creek line become necessary.

Meade spent most of the morning of July 2 attending to matters on Cemetery and Culp's hills. The latter was of particular concern due to its proximity to the Baltimore Pike, which connected the Army of the Potomac to its supply base at Westminster. Meade assigned defense of this critical position to Slocum's Twelfth Corps upon its arrival early on the morning of the second. After getting his men in place, Slocum suggested to Meade that once the Fifth and Sixth Corps arrived, they should assist the Twelfth Corps in an attack against the Confederate position facing Culp's Hill. Meade liked the idea, as a successful attack in that sector would secure the Baltimore Pike and might even create an opportunity for enveloping the rebel left. He told Slocum and Warren to inspect the ground in front of Culp's Hill to determine whether an attack would be feasible. After a quick reconnaissance, however, Slocum and Warren reported that the terrain was too rugged for an attack from Culp's Hill to be successful, which effectively killed whatever hopes Meade had for taking the offensive on July 2.

Nonetheless, Meade was confident. With Slocum's Twelfth Corps occupying Culp's Hill, Howard on Cemetery Hill, the First Corps (now under the command of Maj. Gen. John Newton, who Meade had placed in command after deciding Doubleday, who as senior division commander had led the corps after Reynolds's death, would not do) and Hancock's Second Corps in position on Cemetery Ridge, with the rest of the Third, as well as all of the Fifth and Sixth Corps on the way, he was sure he could handle whatever Lee might throw at him on July 2.

When all of Sickles's Third Corps was finally on hand, Meade ordered that it extend the Federal line south along Cemetery Ridge and take a position from which it could protect two prominent hills, Round Top and Little Round Top. However, once in his designated place Sickles decided that he did not like it one bit. Looking out to the west, he noticed some higher ground located around a peach orchard and at around 11:00 A.M., went to Meade's headquarters to complain about his position. Meade, who was still preoccupied with the situation on Culp's and Cemetery Hills, sent Hunt over to Sickles's headquarters. After looking over the terrain and talking with Sickles, Hunt returned to headquarters and informed Meade that he had told Sickles to keep his command where it was and not advance westward.

Meanwhile, having determined to let Lee make the first move if there was to be any fighting that day, Meade continued positioning his corps, secure that the natural strength of his position would enable him to deal with any contingency. At approximately 3:00 P.M., Sedgwick's Sixth Corps began arriving after a grueling thirty-two mile march from Manchester, Maryland. With the concentration of his army almost complete, Meade decided to call his corps commanders to headquarters to discuss their options.

By then, however, there had been an unexpected and unwelcome change in the situation. Shortly after 2:00 P.M., Sickles, without advising General Hancock, commander of the Second Corps to his right, or army headquarters, had decided to defy Meade's instructions and moved his corps forward to occupy the high ground around the Peach Orchard. Meade first learned of Sickles's actions when one of Warren's aides rode up to his headquarters and reported what was happening. Meade immediately instructed Maj. Gen. George Sykes to move his Fifth Corps up to cover the key positions Sickles's move left exposed. He also instructed Warren to go over to Little Round Top to check on the state of affairs on that key piece of terrain.

Meade then rode forward to the Trostle Farm where Sickles had established his headquarters. Meade found the Third Corps commander in the valley between the Trostle Farm and the Peach Orchard and immediately demanded an explanation for his actions. Sickles stated that he had moved forward in order to take advantage of the higher ground at

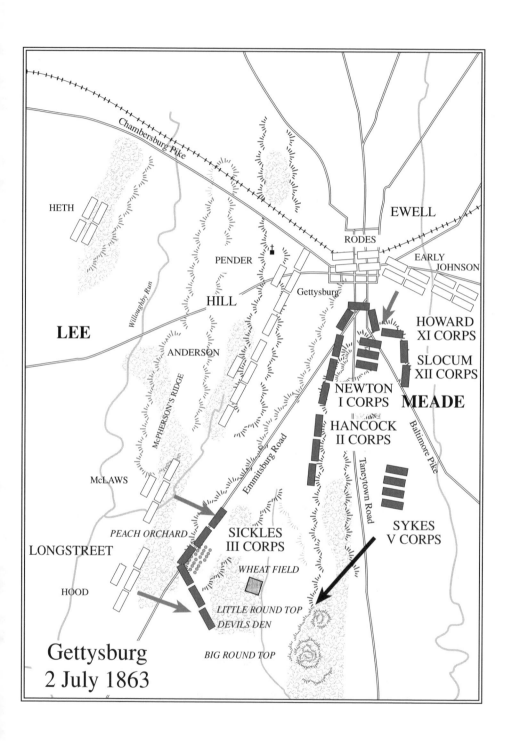

Gettysburg
2 July 1863

the Peach Orchard. Meade, in exasperation over this defiance of his orders, replied: "General Sickles, this is in some respects higher ground . . . but there is still higher in front of you, and if you keep on advancing you will find constantly higher ground all the way to the mountains." A chastened Sickles appeared to accept his commander's logic and replied, "Very well, sir, I'll withdraw then." Just then, however, a Confederate artillery shell slammed into the ground nearby. "I wish to God you could," Meade shouted as he attempted to steady his nervous mount, "but those people will not permit it."[14]

As he rode away from Sickles's command post, Meade encountered a courier from Warren informing him that he had found Little Round Top devoid of Federal troops, and that the rebels were preparing to storm the position. Meade responded by directing that Brig. Gen. Andrew Humphreys's division from the Third Corps be sent to Warren. But almost as soon as he had issued these orders, a second message arrived from Warren assuring him that units from the Fifth Corps were arriving on Little Round Top. Meade decided to keep Humphreys's command with Sickles.

As Meade was attempting to shore up his positions on Little Round Top and at the Peach Orchard, at four p.m. James Longstreet's powerful Confederate First Corps launched a massive assault on the Union left. The arrival of the Fifth Corps managed to save Little Round Top from the Confederate onslaught, although it was a near-run thing. At the Peach Orchard, however, Sickles's line was completely shattered, creating the very real danger that the Union army might be cut in two. Meade personally witnessed the disintegration of Sickles's command and immediately began shifting forces from his center and right to plug the gap in his line created by the Third Corps's defeat. For a few anxious moments, however, Meade and four members of his staff were all that stood in the gap between the Second and Third Corps. Then, just as Confederate forces began advancing toward his position, two divisions from the First Corps arrived and were ordered into the fight by Meade personally.

Meanwhile, at Meade's direction, Hancock had begun taking direct control of the fighting on Cemetery Ridge. Once again, Hancock and the men of the Army of the Potomac came through at Gettysburg. By dark, they had stabilized the situation and secured the center of the Federal line, which at the end of the day ran like a fishhook from Little Round Top north to Cemetery Hill and from Cemetery Hill east to Culp's Hill. The fighting on July 2 finally came to an end when Federal forces on Culp's Hill repulsed an evening attack.

John Gibbon

Born Pennsylvania 1827; although born in the North, Gibbon was raised in North Carolina and appointed to the U.S. Military Academy from that state; graduated in 1847 twentieth in his class of thirty-eight, he was posted to artillery; he saw service in the Mexican War, against the Seminoles in Florida, on the Western frontier, and as an artillery instructor at West Point, rising through the ranks to captain in 1859; the sectional crisis hit the Gibbon family hard—his wife was from Baltimore and three of his brothers joined the Confederacy; Gibbon, though, remained in the Federal army; early in the war he served as chief of artillery for General Irvin McDowell, and later for the First Corps, Army of the Potomac; entering the volunteer organization as brigadier general in May 1862, he took command of the 4th Brigade, First Division, Third Corps, Army of Virginia—the famous "Black Hats" or "Iron Brigade," which he led in the Second Bull Run Campaign; the brigade transferred to the First Corps, Army of the Potomac, and again distinguished itself during the Antietam Campaign in September 1862; he commanded the Second Division in General John Reynolds' First Corps at Fredericksburg, where he was wounded; returning to duty as

Meade knew that Lee could not be satisfied with what he had accomplished so far at Gettysburg and that there was no reason to expect July 3 would be a quiet day. Therefore, once the fighting ended on July 2, Meade called his corps commanders to headquarters for a council of war. As his subordinates gathered at the Leister House, Meade asked them whether they thought the army should stay where it was or withdraw. Although the fighting of the past two days had left some shaken, most of the men assembled saw no reason to withdraw.

commander of the Second Division in General Winfield Scott Hancock's Second Corps, he fought at Chancellorsville in May 1863 and in July at Gettysburg, where he temporarily headed the corps; severely wounded during the heavy action on the third day, he was out of action for several months; after some recruiting duty, he rejoined his command for the Overland Campaign of 1864 and was elevated to major general U.S. Volunteers in June; given command of the Twenty-fourth Corps, Army of the James, in January 1865, he led the corps through the closing stages of the war; one of the officers appointed to receive the surrender of General Robert E. Lee's Army of Northern Virginia, Gibbon was mustered out of the volunteer organization in January 1866; brevetted through major general in the regular army, he became colonel of the 36th Infantry and in 1869 took charge of the 7th Infantry, with which he relieved the surviving portions of Colonel George Armstrong Custer's 7th Cavalry at the Little Big Horn in 1876; he saw considerable service on the Western frontier until promoted to brigadier general in 1885; he retired in 1891; General Gibbon died at Baltimore in 1896 and was buried at Arlington National Cemetery; one of the army's most capable officers, he also wrote an influential artillery manual; his *Personal Recollections of the Civil War* was published posthumously. Early in 1860, when Gibbon was in garrison at Charleston, he and J.J. Pettigrew became friends; Gibbon offered considerable advice and assistance in Pettigrew's efforts to upgrade the South Carolina militia. Pettigrew may or may not have been aware of it at the time, but Gibbon commanded one of the divisions on Cemetery Ridge that he and his men attacked on July 3, 1863, during the Battle of Gettysburg.

They also believed that the army should remain on the defensive, at least until it was clear what Lee's intentions were. With the council having essentially confirmed his own sense of the situation, Meade dismissed his subordinates. Moreover, as they began leaving the building, Meade felt certain of what would happen the next day. Consequently, he made a point of speaking one-on-one with Brig. Gen. John Gibbon, commander of the units holding the center of the line on Cemetery Ridge. "If Lee attacks tomorrow," Meade advised Gibbon, "it will be in *your front.*"[15]

Early the next morning, Meade was back in the saddle looking over the situation. What he saw did little to shake his confidence in the decisions he had made the night before. His general plan for the day, he told Hancock, would be to await a Confederate attack and then, once it was repulsed, to counterattack with the Fifth and Sixth Corps. First, however, Meade decided that the units from Ewell's corps that had seized a section of the Union trench line on Culp's Hill had to be dealt with. At dawn on July 3, Slocum had a hot fight with Ewell's corps in which Union forces effectively restored their position on Culp's Hill, which greatly alleviated Meade's anxiety regarding the Army of the Potomac's supply line on the Baltimore Pike.

Meade spent the rest of the morning riding along his lines and sending out a flurry of orders. Around mid-morning, he encountered Gibbon, who invited him to breakfast. After a leisurely meal of stew, potatoes, and coffee, followed by cigars, at around 12:30 Meade once again mounted his horse and rode off. A little over a half-hour later, Confederate artillery began firing. Meade's prediction for the day's battle was about to be tested.

For approximately an hour, Confederate guns pounded the Federal position on Cemetery Ridge. Having attacked the Federal right and left the previous day, Lee suspected Meade's position might be weak in the center. Unfortunately, for the Confederates and the Widow Leister, their artillery fire was poorly aimed and most of their ordnance sailed over the Union front line to where the Leister House was. After a few shells crashed into the house, and nearly being struck himself, Meade decided to relocate his headquarters to Power's Hill.

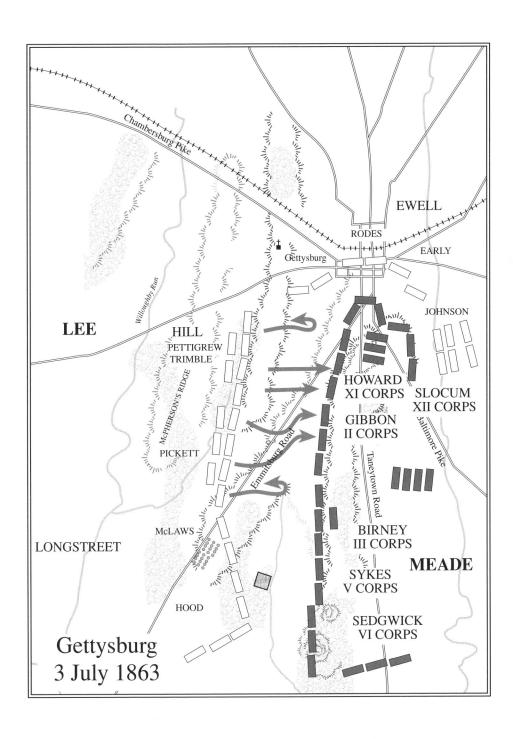

Chambersburg Pike

EWELL

RODES

EARLY

Gettysburg

JOHNSON

LEE

HILL

PETTIGREW
TRIMBLE

Willoughby Run

McPHERSON'S RIDGE

HOWARD
XI CORPS

SLOCUM
XII CORPS

GIBBON
II CORPS

PICKETT

Emmitsburg Road

Baltimore Pike

McLAWS

LONGSTREET

Taneytown Road

BIRNEY
III CORPS

MEADE

SYKES
V CORPS

HOOD

SEDGWICK
VI CORPS

Gettysburg
3 July 1863

Shortly after Meade arrived at Power's Hill, the Confederate infantry began their attack. Sensing a slackening of Union artillery fire (which in fact was a conscious decision the Federals made in order to conserve ammunition for the infantry attack they knew was sure to follow the bombardment), Lee ordered three infantry divisions to advance against the Federal line. Their target was a copse of trees located, as Meade had predicted, on the portion of the Federal line held by Gibbon's command on Cemetery Ridge.

When word of the Confederate infantry attack reached Power's Hill, Meade ordered reserves from the Sixth Corps to move to Gibbon's support and rode forward to Cemetery Ridge. As Meade was leaving Power's Hill, 15,000 Confederates from A.P. Hill's and Longstreet's corps closed on the Federal line. Gibbon's men, anticipating a repeat of the Fredericksburg debacle in reverse, eagerly poured a deadly fire into the enemy's ranks. Despite taking heavy fire, some of the rebels managed to reach the Federal line and achieve a brief penetration as Gibbon, Hancock, and Brig. Gen. Alexander Webb went down wounded. Before Meade and the reserves he had ordered forward could arrive on the scene, however, the rebels had begun falling back.

The suddenness with which the rebel tide subsided stunned Meade. When he reached Gibbon's position, artillerist Frank Haskell informed him, "the enemy's attack is repulsed," Meade was incredulous. *"What?"* he asked, *"is the assault already repulsed?"* Haskell assured him that the rebel attack had indeed failed. Meade immediately turned from Haskell to take in the scene and then remarked, *"Thank God."*[16]

After a quick ride along the line, however, it became evident to the general that his plan to immediately follow up Lee's repulse with a counterattack might not be feasible. Once victory had been assured on Cemetery Ridge, Meade decided to ride over to Little Round Top and talk with Warren. But as Meade turned his horse southward, officers and men began crowding around him, cheering and trying to shake his hand. After making his way through this scene, Meade managed to reach Warren and instructed him to move forward

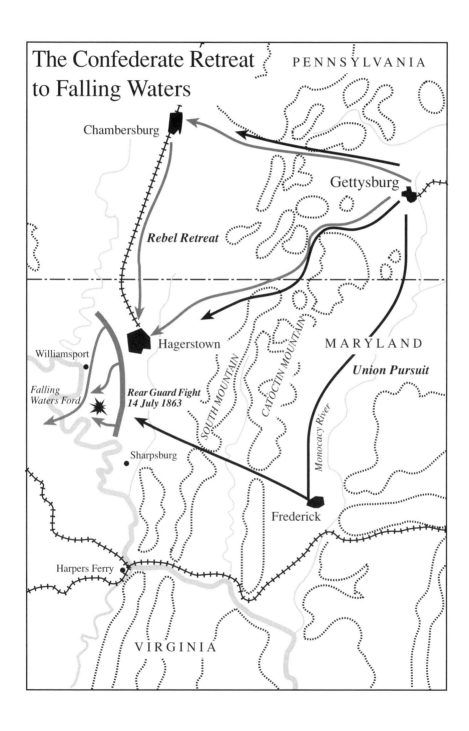

The Confederate Retreat to Falling Waters

PENNSYLVANIA

Chambersburg

Gettysburg

Rebel Retreat

Hagerstown

MARYLAND

Williamsport

Union Pursuit

Falling
Waters Ford

*Rear Guard Fight
14 July 1863*

SOUTH MOUNTAIN

CATOCTIN MOUNTAIN

Monocacy River

Sharpsburg

Frederick

Harpers Ferry

VIRGINIA

ANDREW A. HUMPHREYS

Born Philadelphia 1810; graduated U.S. Military Academy 1831, thirteenth out of a class of thirty-three; brevetted 2d Lieutenant in 2d Artillery; served in Second Seminole War; in 1838 appointed 1st Lieutenant in Corps of Topographical Engineers; spent much of the prewar years engaged in hydrographical surveys of the Mississippi Delta; in November 1861 assigned to General George McClellan's staff; promoted to brigadier general of volunteers in April 1862; during the Peninsula Campaign served as the chief topographical engineer for the Army of the Potomac; in September 1862 assumed command of a division of new recruits in the V Corps; saw little action during the Maryland Campaign; at Fredericksburg his division was a part of the doomed assault on Marye's Heights, there his personal bravery and that of his troops won him much respect; was not involved in the heavy fighting at Chancellorsville; soon after his division was disbanded and he was transferred to take command of a division in General Daniel Sickles's III Corps; turned down a request from General Meade to become the army's chief of staff, preferring to remain in the field; on the second day of the Battle of Gettysburg he fought bravely in Sickles's advanced position against Longstreet's assaults; promoted to major general on July 8, 1863; that same day he became the chief of staff of the Army of the Potomac; performed ably as such until November 25, 1864, when he was appointed to replace Winfield S. Hancock as the commander of the II Corps; led it though the final engagements of the war including Hatcher's Run, White Oak Road, Sutherland Station, and Sayler's Creek; after Appomattox continued his career with the Corps of Engineers until his retirement in 1879; died 1883 and buried in Washington, DC.

from Little Round Top to see if anything could be done to exploit the victory already achieved. Warren promptly pushed three brigades forward, but by the time they had reclaimed the ground lost by Sickles the previous day, it was too late to launch a major counteroffensive. After sending off a message to Washington announcing the results of the day's battle, Meade found a boulder to sit on. Exhausted by the past three days' labors, he soon fell asleep.

Once again, Meade was up early on July 4. While he was slumbering on his boulder, the heavens had opened up and unleashed a drenching rain and thunderstorm. Unable to sleep, Meade got up and began looking over the situation. Lee, he quickly learned, was still in position over on Seminary Ridge. But Meade had no intention of repeating Lee's "bad example . . . in ruining himself attacking a strong position" across an open field. Thus, he decided to spend the fourth resting his men and letting them recuperate a bit from their labors of the past three days. Unfortunately, he also decided to issue a poorly worded order to his army congratulating it on its accomplishments and advising, "Our task is not yet accomplished and the commanding general looks . . . for greater efforts to drive from our soil every vestige of the presence of the invader."[17]

Meade's message, once it arrived at the Executive Mansion, infuriated Lincoln, who was eager that the Union army take advantage of Lee's crossing the Potomac and strike him a decisive blow far from Richmond. The president turned to Halleck and ordered him to get Meade moving to exploit his victory. "If General Meade can complete his work, so gloriously prosecuted thus far, by the literal or substantial destruction of Lee's army," an anxious Lincoln advised Halleck, "the rebellion will be over." But, he also complained, it seemed that Meade's behavior "appear[s] to me to be connected with a purpose to . . . get the enemy across the river again without a further collision, and they do not appear connected with a purpose to prevent his crossing and to destroy him. . . . I did not like the phrase . . . 'Drive the invaders from our soil.'"[18]

When it became evident that Lee was retreating, Meade immediately issued orders for a pursuit to the Potomac. He instructed Sedgwick to take his Sixth Corps and advance in order to determine what Lee was doing and discover the best route for the army to take. By the end of July 5, Sedgwick had reached Fairfield Pass at South Mountain and was probing Rebel defenses there. Unfortunately, a blunder by Butterfield in issuing orders to the Third and Fifth Corps resulted in delays getting forces to Sedgwick's support, and this led to his ouster as chief of staff. When the army reached Frederick, Maryland, Meade tapped Brig. Gen. Andrew Humphreys as Butterfield's replacement. With his command once again firmly in hand, Meade pushed it through heavy rains and over muddy roads in the direction of Williamsport. There, with his back to the swollen Potomac River, Lee was preparing a formidable defensive position.

By July 12, the Army of the Potomac had pushed beyond Hagerstown, Maryland. There Meade established his head-quarters before riding forward to catch his first glimpse of Lee's line. The pressure from Washington had reached a fever pitch. Telegrams had been constantly arriving from Halleck urging Meade not to pass up what the president per-ceived to be a golden opportunity to destroy Lee's army. Meade, accompanied by Humphreys and Warren, did not get a good look at the Rebel position, however, for stormy weather cut short the reconnaissance. He did, however, decide to call his corps commanders together to let them know that, despite the lack of information, he would attack the Confederates the next day if they approved the plan. Only two did. Thus, Meade decided to conduct another reconnaissance before acting. The next day a message arrived from Halleck stating Washington's opinion: "You are strong enough to attack and defeat the enemy before he can effect a crossing. Act upon your own judgment and make your generals execute your orders. Call no council of war. It is proverbial that councils of war never fight. . . . Do not let the enemy escape."[19]

Despite further heavy rains the next day, Meade rode out to conduct another examination of the enemy position. He learned little, however, as visibility remained extremely limited due to the poor weather. Nonetheless, he decided to attack the following morning.

But Meade would not have the opportunity to make his attack. On the night of the thirteenth, Lee crossed the Potomac. When Federal skirmishers moved forward early on the fourteenth to initiate Meade's attack, they found the Rebels gone. Although aware that he would surely catch hell from Washington for not attacking, Meade's anxiety over his decision not to attack dissipated after his trained engineer's eye inspected the Confederate works. Lee had, in fact, constructed an extremely formidable set of defenses that even with the best of weather could have only been taken through a very bloody assault—if at all.

Further salving Meade's conscience was the fact that West Point–trained officers, whose military opinion he respected (such as Humphreys, Sedgwick, Warren, and Hunt), all came away from their inspections convinced that Meade's discretion and Lee's retreat had spared the army another Fredericksburg. "An assault would have been disastrous to us," Hunt believed. "People at home of course will now pitch into Meade, as they did McClellan after Antietam," one officer who shared the high command's resentment of Washington strategists wrote in his diary after making his own inspection. "My own opinion is that under the circumstances . . . [Meade] was justified in putting off his attack. . . . [T]heir line of works . . . were by far the strongest I have seen yet."[20]

Although completely ignorant as to the strength of Lee's defenses at Williamsport, Lincoln did not share the sentiments of Meade's subordinates. In fact, he was furious. "There is," the president complained after learning of Lee's escape, "bad faith somewhere. . . . We had them within our grasp. We had only to stretch forth our hands and they were ours." He then sat down and penned a bitter message for Meade. "I do not believe," Lincoln wrote, "you appreciate the magnitude of the misfortune involved in Lee's escape. . . . He was in your easy grasp, and to have closed upon him would, in connection with our other late successes, have ended the war." Instead, he complained, Meade had "stood and let the flood run down, bridges to be built, and the enemy move away at his leisure. . . . Your golden opportunity is gone, and I am distressed immeasurably because if it."[21]

Lincoln decided not to send the letter and, unable to think of anyone else to take Meade's place, chose not to remove the general. Still, it was not difficult for Meade to discern from the tone of the telegrams he was receiving from Halleck that the president was greatly displeased at how he had conducted operations after Gettysburg. "This is exactly what I expected," Meade advised his wife, "unless I did impractical things, fault would be found with me."[22] To make matters worse, the atmosphere in Washington was being further poisoned by the presence of General Sickles, who had made a beeline for the capital after being wounded on July 2 to make sure his version of what had happened that day received a full hearing before anyone else's. Meade's case was further hurt by the fact that Sickles's cronies Joe Hooker and Dan Butterfield were also on the loose, working to rehabilitate their reputations and avenge perceived wrongs.

Despite the shakiness of his standing in Washington, Meade ordered his army across the Potomac the day after Lee had completed his crossing and warily pursued the Rebels south to the Rappahannock River. After establishing his headquarters at Warrenton, Virginia, Meade asked Halleck for guidance as to future operations. After receiving no response to his query, on July 31 he decided to order a mixed force of infantry and cavalry south of the Rappahannock to feel out the enemy's position. Lee responded by falling back to the south side of the Rapidan. "The government," a frustrated Meade complained, "insists on my pursuing and destroying Lee. The former I can do, but the latter will depend on him as much as on me, for if he keeps out of my way, I can't destroy."[23]

As Meade contemplated his next move, Washington instructed him to dispatch a large contingent from his army to New York City to help squelch the riots that erupted there in July. Expiring enlistments in several of his corps and the detachment of several thousand men for service in South Carolina further diminished Meade's strength as he tried to determine how to get at Lee's army. Consequently, the army would spend several weeks of prime campaigning weather stuck between the Rappahannock and Rapidan Rivers, unable to do anything besides patrol and recuperate from its battles of the spring and summer.

5

AUTUMN MANEUVERS

Within a few weeks after Gettysburg, President Lincoln and General Halleck again began prodding Meade to do something against Lee's army. The Confederate decision in early September 1863 to detach James Longstreet's corps from the Army of Northern Virginia for service in Georgia and Tennessee, a move Union intelligence quickly detected, sparked hopes in Washington that Meade might be able to do something despite his depleted ranks. Lincoln thought the proper response was for Meade to harass the Rebel army by moving "upon Lee at once in the manner of general attack, leaving it to developments whether he will make it a real attack." For his part, Halleck suggested to Meade that perhaps "something may be done to weaken [Lee] or force him still further back."[1]

Meade, however, was unable to see how he could accomplish much on his current line of operations. "Lee," he advised Halleck on September 18, "occupies the south bank of the Rapidan, with every available point crowned with artillery, and prepared to dispute the passage. . . . [A] passage can be forced, but it would, undoubtedly, result in a considerable sacrifice." Meade then stated that even if the Army of the Potomac could force its way across the Rapidan, his opponent's plan was evidently "to check and retard my advance as long and wherever he can . . . , [and] I am not in condition to follow Lee to Richmond, and will be less so after being weakened by a severe battle." Meade then suggested that the "very disadvantageous circumstances" under which the Army of the Potomac currently operated could be avoided through a "demonstration on the Peninsula" and by "chang[ing] my base to the Fredericksburg railroad." This, Meade believed, would compel Lee to "retire from my front." Presuming that, for Halleck and Lincoln, "either of these contingencies is out of the question," Meade asked for their "positive sanction" for forcing a fight with Lee in such a poor operational and tactical situation.[2]

Lincoln and Halleck replied immediately. Neither was willing to assume responsibility for telling Meade, in Halleck's words, "when, where, or how to give battle." Nor were they open to his suggestions for creating a more favorable operational situation by shifting his command to Fredericksburg or menacing Lee's rear via the Peninsula. Unwilling to see or debate the merits of Meade's suggestions, they instead accused the general of being too fixated on Richmond instead of the Confederate army. To drive Lee "slowly back into his intrenchments at Richmond, and there to capture him," Lincoln wrote, "is an idea I have been trying to repudiate for quite a year. . . . If our army cannot fall upon the enemy and hurt him where he is, it is plain to me it can gain nothing by attempting to follow him over a succession of intrenched lines into a fortified city." They also suggested that if Meade did not think he could successfully undertake offensive operations against Lee where he was, then perhaps he should fall back closer to Washington and assume the defensive. This would allow authorities to more productively employ a large contingent of the Army of the Potomac elsewhere.[3]

Lincoln's and Halleck's responses were about as unhelpful as Meade expected. Nonetheless, unwilling to accept stalemate and its possible consequences, Meade decided on September 21 to have General Buford take his cavalry up the Rapidan to examine the possibility of turning Lee's left. Before Buford could complete his reconnaissance, however, Meade was summoned to Washington. He arrived shortly before midnight on September 22 and learned the administration was considering detaching forces from the Army of the Potomac and sending them to Tennessee to help the Army of the Cumberland, then trapped in Chattanooga after its defeat at Chickamauga. Meade protested on the grounds that he thought Buford's movements held promise, and he told Lincoln and Halleck that if they were acting on a belief that "I was too slow or prudent, to put some one else in my place." Halleck dismissed the latter suggestion out of hand, and Meade left Washington the following afternoon under the impression that "the President was satisfied" with his arguments against diminishing the strength of the Army of the Potomac.[4]

Upon returning to his headquarters, Meade spirits were further lifted when he learned that Buford's reconnaissance had gone well. His hopes for developing this into something more were dashed, however, when at 3:00 A.M. on September 24, orders arrived from Halleck directing him to "prepare the Eleventh and Twelfth Corps to be sent to Washington, as soon as cars can be sent to you."[5] Eight hours later Meade issued orders directing Generals Howard and Slocum to take their commands to the capital. By the evening of September 27, both corps were on trains headed for Tennessee.

It did not take long for Lee to figure out that he now faced a considerably diminished foe and to begin looking for a way to exploit the situation. Almost as soon as he learned of Washington's move, he decided to attempt a repeat of his smashing success of the previous summer at Second Manassas. Much like John Pope's army had been, Lee recognized that Meade's logistical dependence on the Orange and Alexandria Railroad made him vulnerable to a turning movement to the west. To take advantage of this, Lee decided to try to move around the Federal right and threaten the Orange and Alexandria. This, he believed, would force the Army of the Potomac into the open and set up "an opportunity to strike a blow."[6]

Federal cavalry picked up evidence of the Confederate move almost as soon as it began, and once their reports reached headquarters, Meade easily divined his enemy's intentions. Unlike Pope, Meade would give the Rebel commander no opening for a decisive stroke. He instructed his army to about-face, march north along the railroad, and not to stop until it had crossed Bull Run. In addition, he ordered the preparation of strong defenses at Centreville from which the army could deal with anything the Confederates might try. Through forced marches, the Army of the Potomac quickly negated Lee's head start in the race for Bull Run.

By the afternoon of October 14, all but Warren's Second Corps had forded Broad Run on the way to the Bull Run crossings. As he moved toward the Orange and Alexandria, Lt. Gen. A.P. Hill, commander of the Confederate Third Corps, spotted Sykes's Fifth Corps crossing Broad Run just east of Bristoe Station. Impetuously, Hill decided to strike a blow at the apparently isolated command as it negotiated the stream.

Hill's advance nicely set up his own command for an ambush by Warren's corps as it moved along the railroad embankment. The Confederate corps was shattered, and upon learning that Warren was engaged, Meade ordered the Third and First Corps to march back to Bristoe Station to aid him. By the time they arrived, however, the fight was over and the bloodied Confederates had pulled back. Deciding he could do no more, Meade ordered a resumption of the army's concentration at Centreville. After testing the strong Federal lines there and finding that Meade had frustrated his attempt to compel the Army of the Potomac to fight at a disadvantage, Lee decided he had no alternative but to fall back to the Rappahannock. Meade followed close behind but was unable to bring Lee to battle, and by October 20, the Army of the Potomac was back at Warrenton.

Although he had successfully thwarted Lee's maneuver, Meade found himself bombarded with complaints from

Washington about his conduct of the campaign. The general admitted he was disappointed that he had not been able to catch the Rebels at a disadvantage, but he was satisfied with his performance. "It was greatly in my interest to fight," he advised his wife after the campaign, "and I was most anxious to do so, but I would not do so with all the advantages on his side. . . . There is no doubt my failure to engage Lee in battle during his recent advance created great disappointment, in which feeling I fully share."[7]

Meade's expectation that the administration would find fault was correct. Halleck even went so far as to let Meade know on October 18 that it was the administration's belief that "Lee is plainly bullying you." And, in response to Meade's desire not to try and provoke a clash until he had a good picture of Lee's whereabouts and intentions, Halleck opined that all the general had to do was "pursue and fight him" in order to "find out where he is." Halleck's implication that the failure to bring Lee to battle was due not to circumstances, but to a lack of moral courage on Meade's part, infuriated the general. After receiving a faultfinding letter from Halleck, Meade turned to an aide and remarked in frustration, "If Bob Lee will go into those fields there and fight me, man for man, I will do it this afternoon."[8]

Finally, Meade decided he had taken about all he could stand from the armchair strategists in Washington. "I must insist," he informed Halleck, "on being spared the inflictions of such truisms in the guise of opinions as you have recently honored me with, particularly as they were not asked for." He closed his letter by stating that if Washington was in fact so dissatisfied with his generalship, then "I ought to be . . . and desire to be, relieved from command."[9]

Halleck replied by stating that he had not meant to give offense but merely to give Meade a sense of the growing dissatisfaction among Washington politicians and the Northern public with his generalship. This somewhat mollified Meade personally but did nothing to silence the growing chorus of discontent in the capital, fueled in part by a whispering campaign by Dan Sickles, whose antagonism toward Meade received further fuel when his request for restoration to command of the Third Corps was flatly rejected.

Lincoln was indeed bitterly disappointed with Meade's performance as commander of the Army of the Potomac and in agreement with those who were complaining that he was too much of a "McClellan general" to conduct the sort of aggressive, offensive operations the public and administration demanded. Further trying the administration's patience was the general's reluctance in late September to quash efforts by a number of high-ranking officers to circulate a testimonial "expressing the high opinion they had of McClellan as a man, and the attachment they still felt for him as their old commander."[10]

Yet Lincoln kept Meade in command. In part, this was because the president recognized the general still enjoyed considerable public prestige from his victory at Gettysburg. It was also clear that the Army of the Potomac was satisfied with Meade and had little stomach for yet another change in command. An officer in the Fifth Corps spoke for many when he wrote his brother after Bristoe Station: "You *astound* me with the rumour that Genl. Meade is to be removed. Great Scott! What in the world do the authorities want? . . . Candidly, we feel every confidence in Meade, and if anyone succeeds him but McClellan, the dissatisfaction will be intense."[11]

Perhaps most important in keeping Lincoln from firing Meade was the fact that there really was no acceptable alternative from either a military or political standpoint. Much of the army, of course, still longed for McClellan's return, but that was politically out of the question. It was also clear that neither the officers nor the rank and file of the Army of the Potomac would accept Joseph Hooker's return or the appointment of an outsider. Unfortunately for Lincoln, all of the possible candidates within the Army of the Potomac had major liabilities. The most promising, Winfield Scott Hancock, was still recuperating from a horrible Gettysburg wound; Warren and John Sedgwick were both unreconstructed McClellan men; and George Sykes, John Newton, and William French had done nothing to suggest they were capable of handling an entire army.

Still, relations between Meade and Washington were extremely tense, and a late October meeting between the general, Lincoln, and Halleck did little to improve matters. Meade found Lincoln manifestly "disappointed that I had not got a battle out of Lee" but unwilling to find fault, though skeptical regarding how much could be accomplished in the near future. As was his wont, Halleck played the heavy and made it clear to Meade that he believed it "was very urgent that something should be done." Meade complained, "What that something was, he did not define."[12] Although possibly successful in deflecting Meade's growing exasperation away from the president, the commander left these meetings with Lincoln and Halleck with no clear guidance as to what exactly the administration wanted or expected from him.

The first matter to which Meade devoted his attention after leaving Washington was logistics. Although he personally was able to reach Warrenton quickly and establish headquarters after Bristoe Station, the Orange and Alexandria Railroad, his principal supply line, was in shambles; Lee had torn it up while falling back from Centreville. Consequently, Meade did not anticipate his army would be in good shape logistically until the railroad was repaired, for there was no way 90,000 men could subsist off of an area two armies had occupied and fought over for more than a year. *"The whole country is a barren waste,"* one officer wrote as the army moved south along the Orange and Alexandria. "You cannot imagine the distress of the inhabitants in this part of Virginia. *Starvation stares them in the face."* One man wrote after the war: "The newspapers at the north that condemned the delay at Brandy Station, and sneered at the idea that the army needed a base of supplies, simply exhibited their profound ignorance of the first principles of campaigning. . . . [O]ur army was now to march into a wilderness where even a regiment could not find subsistence."[13]

As he awaited completion of repair work on the Orange and Alexandria, Meade contemplated what he wanted to do with his army once the line was secure. Of one thing he was certain, though: the overland route along the Orange and

Alexandria was still the wrong one for the Army of the Potomac to be taking in its operations against Lee. While it might preclude any prospect of Lee threatening Washington, that area remained woefully unpromising for conducting offensive operations. Echoing the complaints of his chief, one of Meade's staff officers laid out the enduring problem for his wife. "We can easily whip Lee if we can only get at him, but that is the trouble," he complained, "he of course will fall back to Richmond, destroying as he retreats the whole line. If we follow him . . . , we have three rivers to cross all of which are defensible, and with a small force can delay us much. There is nothing to forage upon in this country, and the question is how are we to get supplies. . . . If Lee at any time chooses to attack he can advance and compel us to fall back by turning this position."[14]

On November 2, though not optimistic of the prospects of its being adopted, Meade submitted to Halleck a new plan that proposed adopting another line of operations. Instead of advancing along the Orange and Alexandria, Meade suggested "throwing the whole army rapidly and secretly across the Rappahannock at Banks' Ford and Fredericksburg, and taking position on the heights beyond the town."[15] From there the army could advance to a point south of Fredericksburg, from where an advance on Richmond could be supported first by the Richmond, Fredericksburg, and Potomac Railroad, then by the rivers of the Virginia tidewater.

Halleck and Lincoln, to no one's surprise—certainly not Meade's—quickly vetoed the plan. On November 3 Halleck advised the general that Lincoln "does not see that the proposed change of base is likely to produce [a] favorable result, while its disadvantages are manifest. I have fully concurred. . . . Any tactical movement to turn a flank or threaten a communication is left to your own judgment; but an entire change of base under existing circumstances I can neither advise nor approve."[16]

Although disappointed at Halleck's response, Meade accepted the president's decision and quickly made plans to make the best of what was available. Although reconstruction

JOHN SEDGWICK

Born Connecticut 1813; received his early education in the Connecticut common schools and a few months at an academy; he taught school before entering the U.S. Military Academy, from which he graduated twenty-fourth in his class in 1837; appointed 2d lieutenant in the 2d Artillery in 1837; promoted to 1st lieutenant in 1839; par-

ticipated in the Seminole War, assisted in moving the Cherokee Indians west of the Mississippi, served on the northern frontier during the Canadian border disturbances, and on various garrison assignments; participated in the Mexican War; brevetted captain for gallant conduct in the battles of Contreras and Churubusco and major for gallant conduct in the action at Chapultepec; promoted to captain in 1849; after several years of garrison duty, he welcomed his appointment as major in the newly organized 1st Cavalry in 1855; participated in the Utah Expedition of 1857–58, and in the warfare with the Kiowa and Comanche Indians, 1858–60; in 1861 he enjoyed quick promotions to lieutenant colonel of the 2d Cavalry, colonel of the 1st Cavalry, colonel of the 4th Cavalry, and finally brigadier general of volunteers; important assignments followed as brigade and then division commander in the Army of the Potomac; in 1862 he participated in most of the Peninsular Campaign, including Glendale where he was severely wounded; promoted to major general of volunteers in July 1862, he played a prominent role in the Battle of Antietam, where he was again wounded; he commanded for a time the Second Corps and the Ninth Corps, but in 1863 he led the Sixth Corps in the Chancellorsville, Fredericksburg, Salem Heights, Gettysburg, Rappahannock Station, and the Mine Run operations; in 1864, still commanding the Sixth Corps, he fought in the Wilderness and was killed by a Confederate sniper while directing the placing of artillery at Spotsylvania. Much loved by his men, this strict disciplinarian, a generous and affable bachelor, known to his troops as "Uncle John," was an able corps commander. He is buried in his native town, Cornwall Hollow, Connecticut.

efforts on the Orange and Alexandria were not yet complete,
Meade had already fixed his eye on Confederate redoubts
north of the Rappahannock at Kelly's Ford and Rappahannock
Station. An attack on these positions, he decided, at least
offered the opportunity for offensive operations that would satisfy Washington and might even provoke Lee to come out of his
strong positions and fight in the open, all without entailing too
much risk for the Army of the Potomac.

On November 7 Meade ordered General Sedgwick to attack
at Rappahannock Station with the Fifth and Sixth Corps and
Maj. Gen. William French to attack Kelly's Ford with the Third,
Second, and First Corps. The Federal strikes were complete
tactical successes. Both Confederate positions were overrun,
with Sedgwick capturing over fifteen hundred prisoners and
French taking over four hundred. The operation provided an
immediate morale boost to the army, and to his delight, Meade
received enthusiastic cheering from his men. "They closed
around him and cheered lustily, throwing caps in the air and
fairly mobbing him," one soldier wrote in his diary. "Meade . . .
seems to be steadily winning his way into their confidence and
many favorable comments are heard among the rank and file
as to his ability to handle them." As gratifying as the cheers
were, Meade nonetheless was "greatly disappointed" that Lee
had not put up more of a fight, for he was "most desirous of
effecting something decisive."[17]

Meade decided to follow up his victories by pushing both
wings forward to Brandy Station in hopes of catching Lee and
forcing him to fight in the open field. Unfortunately, on
November 8 thick fog impeded Federal efforts to get across
the Rappahannock in force and figure out what the Rebels
were doing. Once the weather cleared, assuming Lee would
make a stand at Brandy Station, Meade ordered his men forward, but they found nothing until they reached the Rapidan
River. Lee, to the disappointment of Meade and his subordinates, had slipped away to the high ground on the river's
southern bank. Still, Lincoln was very pleased with what had
been accomplished at Rappahannock Station and Kelly's Ford,
and even sent a letter to Meade "to say: 'well done.'"[18]

WILLIAM H. FRENCH

Born Maryland 1815; appointed to U.S. Military Academy from the District of Columbia; graduated 1837, twenty-second in his class of fifty cadets that included John Sedgwick, Joseph Hooker, Braxton Bragg, Jubal Early, and John Pemberton; brevetted 2d lieutenant and posted to artillery; served in Seminole wars; 1st lieutenant 1838; won two brevets for gallantry in Mexican War; captain 1848; at the outbreak of the Civil War he commanded the Federal garrison at Eagle Pass, Texas, where he refused to follow General David E. Twiggs in surrendering Federal property to secessionist authorities; led his command to the mouth of the Rio Grande and there embarked for Key West; promoted to major U.S. Army and brigadier general U.S. Volunteers 1861; commanded a brigade in the Second Corps in the Peninsular Campaign and the Third Division of that corps at Antietam; major general U.S. Volunteers November 1862; led his division at Fredericksburg and Chancellorsville; during the Gettysburg Campaign he commanded the District of Harpers Ferry; ascended to command of the Third Corps following the wounding of General Daniel Sickles at Gettysburg; in the fall of 1863 he was criticized by General George G. Meade for his corps' slowness in exploiting a perceived opportunity to trap the enemy during the Mine Run operations; left without a command when the Third Corps was disbanded that winter in the Army of the Potomac reorganization; mustered out of the Volunteer organization in March 1864, he saw no further field service; brevetted through brigadier general U.S. Army for Fair Oaks, Antietam, and Chancellorsville and major general U.S. Army for war service; promoted to the full rank of lieutenant colonel in the regular army 1864; colonel 4th Artillery 1877; having retired from active duty 1880, General French died the following year. Known as a gifted artillerist, he had demonstrated solid command ability before the Mine Run accusations ruined his reputation.

The commander was well aware, though, that the victories of November 7 would not satisfy Washington for long. Thus, as soon as he determined Lee's position south of the Rapidan, he began working on plans to attack it, even though the weather had turned bitterly cold and the mountains just west of Culpeper were already covered with snow. Once repairs on the railroad were complete and sufficient stockpiles of supplies were established, Meade planned to rapidly march his army east from their camps around Brandy Station to Jacobs' Mill, Germanna, and Culpeper Mine Fords on the Rapidan. There the army would cross the river east of the Confederate entrenchments and then swing south and west to either attack Lee's position "or compel him to attack me out of his formidable river entrenchments."[19]

By the last week of November, Meade was ready to carry out a plan that, though well conceived, would be frustrated by terrible friction. First, heavy rains forced a two-day delay that gave the Confederates time to detect the Federal move. These rains also swelled the Rapidan to the point that problems developed with the pontoon bridges. Then, when the operation finally began on November 26, General French, commander of the Third Corps, began his march two hours late and had difficulty figuring out what roads to take after crossing the river. All of these problems frustrated Meade's plan of getting the entire army across the Rapidan and in position to attack Lee from the west by November 27.

The Confederate commander quickly discerned what Meade was up to and shifted his forces east to counter the Federal move. French's difficulties had not affected the movements of Warren's Second Corps, so that unit managed to get into its designated position on the Orange Turnpike near Robertson's Tavern and begin skirmishing with Lee on November 27 as it awaited the arrival of the rest of the army. Unfortunately, French once again encountered problems that day. The division commander at the head of his column proved incapable of negotiating the roads through the thick woods. This allowed a Confederate division to move into position to engage French's corps at Payne's Farm and delay its march to Warren's support long enough for Lee to prepare strong westward-facing positions on the high ground overlooking Mine Run.

For the next two days, Meade and his subordinates probed the Confederate lines in preparation for an assault, enduring a severe rainstorm followed by a dramatic drop in temperature. On the evening of November 29, Meade convened a council of war to consider his options. Although most of the officers assembled were greatly impressed by Lee's position along Mine Run, Warren told Meade that he had conducted a thorough reconnaissance of the Rebel right and "found a position which he considered a good one to attack the enemy from."[20] Trusting Warren's judgment, Meade told him to take his entire corps, as well as two divisions from French's corps and one from Sedgwick's, south and strike the Confederate right at 8:00 A.M. the next morning. While Warren was making his attack, the rest of the army would press Lee's center and left.

When dawn came on a miserably cold November 30, Warren prudently decided to conduct a preliminary reconnaissance of the enemy position in his front. What he found stunned him. The Rebels had taken advantage of the previous night to construct fortifications as formidable as any yet seen in the war. Warren saw that the enemy "line had been re-enforced with all the troops and artillery that could be put in position; the breastworks, epaulements, and abatis perfected, and that a run for eight minutes was the least time our line could have to close the space between us, during which we would be exposed [to] every species of fire." There was no way, his trained engineer mind recognized, that he could carry the enemy works. Thus, he sent an aide, Washington Roebling, to Meade to inform him that the enemy's "position and strength seem so formidable that I advise against making the attack here. The full light of the sun shows me that I cannot succeed."[21]

When Roebling arrived at army headquarters, he found Meade exceedingly anxious to hear the sound of Warren's assault, which was to be the sign for commencing attacks all along the Confederate line. "My God!" Meade responded when Roebling gave him Warren's message, "General Warren has half my army at his disposal!" Meade summoned his horse and

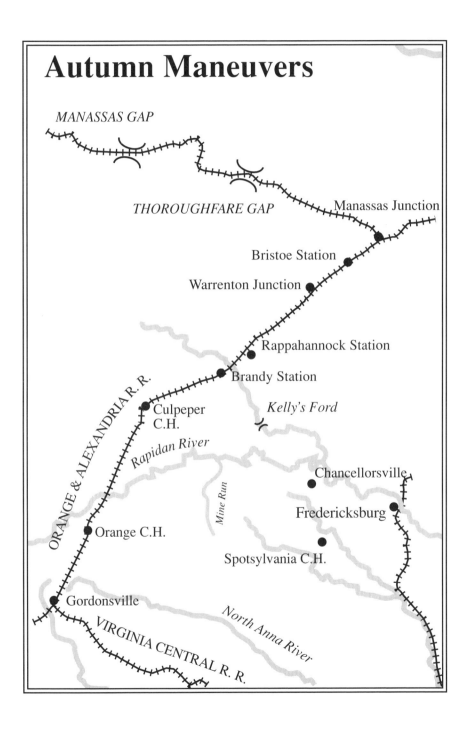

Autumn Maneuvers

MANASSAS GAP

THOROUGHFARE GAP

Manassas Junction

Bristoe Station

Warrenton Junction

Rappahannock Station

Brandy Station

ORANGE & ALEXANDRIA R. R.

Culpeper C.H.

Kelly's Ford

Rapidan River

Chancellorsville

Mine Run

Fredericksburg

Orange C.H.

Spotsylvania C.H.

Gordonsville

North Anna River

VIRGINIA CENTRAL R. R.

rushed to Warren's command post. He arrived there shortly after 10:00 A.M. and immediately realized that his subordinate had made the correct decision. Meade instructed the rest of his command to "suspend the attack until further orders" and returned to headquarters in what one officer described as "the worst possible humor."[22]

Finally deciding that nothing more could be done, Meade withdrew his army across the Rapidan on the night of December 1–2. "But for your disapproval of a change of base," he immediately informed Halleck, "I should, instead of recrossing the Rapidan, have taken up a position in front of Fredericksburg. . . . [T]here was no probability of success in attacking the enemy in his strongly entrenched position."[23] Once back at Brandy Station, the men began construction of winter quarters.

The Army of the Potomac was finished campaigning for the year, but Meade knew that his troubles were anything but over. The decision not to attack Lee at Mine Run was applauded throughout the army, for all who saw the enemy's position agreed, in the words of one member of the Iron Brigade, "To have charged those Heights . . . would have been sheer murder." One officer in the Fifth Corps wrote: "I can truly say there was not an officer or man in the division but that felt it now simply impossible to carry such entrenchments. It could not be done, it were madness to attempt it, worse than at Fredericksburg to allow it." A Pennsylvania colonel concluded, "The army, perhaps the Union cause, was saved, due to the clear judgment and military skill of those grand officers, Meade and Warren."[24]

Meade was nonetheless certain that his failure to attack would displease Washington. In a letter to his wife, written after the army had recrossed the Rapidan, two years of frustration came pouring out as he explained his decision and his feelings on what the consequences might be:

> I, having come to the conclusion that an attack could not be successful, determined to, and did, withdraw the army. I am fully aware it

will be said I did wrong in deciding this question by reasoning, and that I ought to have
tried, and then a failure would have been evidence of my good judgment; but I trust I have
too much reputation as a general to be obliged
to encounter certain defeat in order to prove
that victory was not possible. . . . I would
rather be ignominiously dismissed, and suffer
anything, than knowingly and willfully have
thousands of brave men slaughtered for nothing. . . . My conscience is clear. I did the best I
could. If I had thought there was any reasonable degree of probability of success, I would
have attacked. I did not think so; on the con-
trary, [I] believe it would result in a useless
and criminal slaughter of brave men, and
might result in serious disaster to the army. . . .
There will be a great howl all over the country.
Letter writers and politicians will denounce
me . . . , and finally the Administration will be
obliged to yield to popular clamor and discard
me. For all this I am prepared, fortified . . . by
a clear conscience, and the conviction that I
have acted from a high sense of duty, to
myself as a soldier, to my men as their general, and to my country and its cause, as the
agent having its vital interests solemnly
entrusted to me, which I have no right wan-
tonly to play with and to jeopardize, either for
my own personal benefit, or to satisfy the
demands of popular clamor, or interested
politicians.[25]

When the spring of 1864 arrived, Meade would still have his
head as well as command of the Army of the Potomac, for there
still was no alternative leader available who would be acceptable to both the army and Washington. Meade was correct, however, in his prediction that the operations of the army under his

command would be the subject of "a great howl." With Radical favorites Sickles, Hooker, Abner Doubleday, and Daniel Butterfield on the prowl in the capital and eager to settle scores, it was inevitable that their friends in Congress would take up the task of reexamining the Gettysburg Campaign. Under the leadership of such men as Meade's old nemesis from Michigan, Sen. Zachariah Chandler, the Joint Committee on the Conduct of the War undertook an investigation designed to rehabilitate Hooker and discredit the McClellan clique. Central to this was their effort to fashion an account of the Gettysburg Campaign that was distinctly unfavorable to the commander under whose leadership the Army of the Potomac had won its greatest victory.

In the history of 1863 the Radicals carefully crafted, the Army of the Potomac's operations were the backdrop to an irrepressible conflict between loyal and trustworthy officers whose sought to wage hard, aggressive war against the Rebels and a nefarious band of timid McClellan sympathizers in the army's high command. In the Radical version of the Gettysburg Campaign that emerged from Congress's investigation (based largely on the testimony of Sickles, Hooker, Doubleday, and Butterfield), all of the critical decisions in response to Lee's crossing the Potomac into Maryland were made by Hooker before his removal from command. Meade's only real task after taking command was to, guided by Chief of Staff Butterfield, continue following the plan Hooker had conceived.

Once the armies were engaged, Meade, as was typical of a West Point, McClellan-favored officer, had no taste for battle, and only the actions of fighting generals such as Sickles prevented him from retreating from Gettysburg. Sickles's "heroic" decision to defy his timid commander and advance to the Peach Orchard was portrayed as the critical point in the battle, for it made it impossible for Meade to carry out his desire to retreat on July 2. Had Sickles not been wounded, there would have been a counterbalance to the defensive-minded high command, and the Gettysburg Campaign would have resulted in a quicker and more decisive victory. "I suppose after awhile," Meade mused to his wife after reading of the Radicals' report, "it will be discovered I was not at Gettysburg at all."[26]

In addition to rewriting the history of Gettysburg, Congress also reexamined Chancellorsville. Not surprisingly, Hooker's performance was cast in a highly complimentary light, with blame for the defeat deflected from Fighting Joe to McClellan loyalist John Sedgwick. Only a strenuous appeal by Meade prevented Secretary of War Edwin Stanton, an ally of the Radical Republicans, from relieving Sedgwick.

Meade was unable, however, to prevent the administration from authorizing a foolhardy cavalry raid on Richmond in February 1864. Led by Brig. Gen. Judson Kilpatrick and Col. Ulric Dahlgren, the raid's objective was to dash into the Confederate capital, liberate Federal prisoners held there, and with them take control of the city. The raid, as Meade expected, turned out to be a spectacular failure that cost the Union over three hundred men and did not come close to entering Richmond.

6
WITH GRANT TO THE JAMES

While Kilpatrick and Dahlgren were carrying out their mis-
guided mission, more-promising developments were taking
place. On March 1, 1864, Congress passed a bill reviving the
rank of lieutenant general, and two days later Ulysses S. Grant
was appointed to that rank and accepted the office of commanding general.

Grant arrived in Washington on the afternoon of March 8
and, after a quick meal, headed over to the Executive Mansion
to meet the president. After a whirlwind round of receptions
and meetings, the new lieutenant general decided to pay a visit
to the Army of the Potomac. Grant reached Brandy Station in
the afternoon of the tenth and, escorted by General
Humphreys, headed over to Meade's headquarters.
Accompanying the commanding general was Maj. Gen. William
F. (Baldy) Smith. Smith had impressed Grant at Chattanooga
and was widely rumored to be the man who would replace
Meade if Grant decided a change was necessary.

Grant was well aware of the fact that Meade was in low favor in Washington. A keen observer of political matters with many connections in political and military circles, he knew of the Army of the Potomac's problematic relationship with Republicans in Congress and the administration. And if Grant was not already informed of the basic direction of the ongoing investigations of Gettysburg and other campaigns, General Sickles no doubt had made a point of making Grant aware of which way the political winds were blowing when he encountered him in Washington. Indeed, no less an authority than Secretary of War Edwin Stanton told Grant before he headed down to Brandy Station, "you are going to the Army of the Potomac and you will find a very weak irresolute man there and my advice to you is to make a change at once."[1]

Meade, of course, was well aware of the delicacy of his own position. Moreover, he was so fed up with all the headaches associated with it that he expected and even hoped the burden might be lifted. Consequently, as soon as he had Grant alone, Meade told him "he would be willing to take command of a corps" if the general in chief wanted to place either Halleck or William T. Sherman in command of the Army of the Potomac. "He urged," Grant later wrote, "that the work before us was of such vast importance to the whole nation that the feeling or wishes of no one person should stand in the way of selecting the right men for all positions."[2] Grant was surprised and impressed. He immediately dropped any thought of replacing Meade. Smith would have to settle for command of a corps in Maj. Gen. Benjamin Butler's Army of the James.

Grant and Meade then got down to business. Among the things they discussed was Meade's plan for reorganizing the Army of the Potomac from five corps into three, which Grant immediately approved, and they continued their talks the following day as they traveled together to Washington. "I was very much pleased with Grant," Meade informed his wife. "In the views he expressed to me he showed much more capacity and character than I had expected."[3]

As Meade consolidated the Army of the Potomac's corps, Grant developed strategy for the 1864 campaigns. He planned to target the two main Confederate armies, Gen. Joseph E. Johnston's Army of Tennessee in Georgia and Robert E. Lee's Army of Northern Virginia. His favorite subordinate, Maj. Gen. William T. Sherman, would handle affairs in Georgia, while Grant himself tackled the problem of achieving victory in Virginia.

It was a matter to which Grant had already given some thought. In January 1864 Halleck had asked Grant for his views on the Union effort in the East. The general sent his response, prepared with the assistance of two West Point–trained staff officers whose previous experiences with the Army of the Potomac had soured them on the overland route, to Washington on January 19. Grant asked "whether an abandonment of all previously attempted lines to Richmond is not advisable, and in lieu of these one be taken farther south." He then suggested that the Army of the Potomac not seek bat-

WILLIAM F. SMITH

Nicknamed "Baldy," born Vermont 1824; graduated U.S. Military Academy 1845, fourth out of a class of forty-one; commissioned 2d Lieutenant and assigned to the corps of topographical engineers; spent prewar years engaged in surveys and teaching mathematics at West Point; in 1861 made colonel of the 4th Vermont Volunteers; fought at First Manassas; promoted to brigadier general of volunteers on August 13, 1861; given command of a division in the IV Corps; served at the siege of Yorktown; fought at the battle of Williamsburg and, after his division was transferred to VI Corps, in the Seven Days' Battles; served at Antietam; became commander of VI Corps on November 16, 1862; saw little action at Fredericksburg, though afterward he and General William B. Franklin wrote directly to President Lincoln criticizing Ambrose Burnside's leadership, which along with his friendship with George McClellan led to his removal from

tle with Lee's army along the overland route between Richmond and Washington. Instead, he proposed that 60,000 men from Meade's army be put on boats, sail south to Suffolk, Virginia, and then conduct a massive raid in the direction of Raleigh, North Carolina. This force would especially target the railroads connecting Virginia to the war resources of the rest of the Confederacy, without which it would be impossible for Lee's army to survive. Such operations would, Grant concluded, "draw the enemy from campaigns of their own choosing, and for which they are prepared . . . , [and] virtually force an evacuation of Virginia."[4]

Although Meade and other Army of the Potomac generals would no doubt have seen the merits of Grant's bold plan, it received a cold reception in Washington. Halleck informed Grant that his proposal, and any plan that significantly diminished the forces protecting Washington, was unacceptable. He

command and transfer to IX Corps; during the Gettysburg Campaign he commanded a division of Pennsylvania militia; sent west and served as chief of engineers for the Army of the Cumberland during the Siege of Chattanooga, during which he opened a key supply line known as the "Cracker Line"; this feat, and his service during the assault on Missionary Ridge impressed Ulysses S. Grant. Smith was promoted to major general at Grant's urging on March 9, 1864; transferred to the Army of the James under Benjamin Butler and given command of XVIII Corps, where he feuded with Butler; soon after the corps was transferred to the Army of the Potomac, where it was involved in the bloody and fruitless attack at Cold Harbor, after which Smith began to complain bitterly about the ability of General Meade; in late June at Petersburg his hesitation in attacking lightly-held enemy trenches on June 15 enabled the Confederates to reinforce the town and prepare formidable defenses, thus prolonging the war for another year; afterward his irrepressible penchant for intrigue led to his removal from command on July 19, 1864; spent the rest of the war in non-combat duties; after the war he served as president of the International Ocean Telegraph Company; died 1903 and is buried at Arlington National Cemetery.

ULYSSES S. GRANT

Born Ohio 1822; graduated U.S. Military Academy 1843, twenty-first in his class; brevetted 2d lieutenant in 4th Infantry 1843; 2d lieutenant 1845; 1st lieutenant 1847; regimental quartermaster 1847 to 1853; brevetted captain 1847 for gallant conduct in Mexican War; assigned in 1852 to duty in California, where he missed his wife and drank heavily. Resigned from army in 1854 to avoid court martial; failed at a number of undertakings; appointed colonel 21st Illinois Infantry and then brigadier general volunteers in 1861; major general volunteers 1862; gained national attention following victories at Fort Donelson, Shiloh, and Vicksburg; received thanks of Congress and promotion to major general U.S. Army in 1863; after victories around Chattanooga, appointed lieutenant general and commander of all U.S. forces in 1864. Accompanied Meade's Army of the Potomac on a bloody campaign of attrition through the Wilderness, Spotsylvania, Cold Harbor, siege of Petersburg, and the pursuit to Appomattox; commander of the U.S. Army 1864 to 1869; U.S. president 1869 to 1877. Visited Europe, suffered bankruptcy, and wrote his memoirs while dying of cancer; died in 1885 in New York City, where he is buried. "The art of war is simple enough," Grant once explained. "Find out where your enemy is. Get at him as soon as you can. Strike at him as hard as you can, and keep moving on." A staff officer said of Grant: "His face has three expressions: deep thought, extreme determination, and great simplicity and calmness."

further explained that the administration had determined the best way to accomplish the goal of defeating Lee was to fight him between Washington and "Richmond, on our shortest line of supplies, and in such a position that we can combine our whole force." Unable to concede the arguments of those within and outside the Army of the Potomac that McClellan's

Peninsula Campaign was based on a superior concept operationally, Halleck argued that the history of the war in Virginia so far proved nothing regarding the best line of operations. Thus, he concluded, "we must recur to fundamental principles in regard to interior and exterior lines. . . . [I]f we operate by North Carolina or the Peninsula, we must act with a divided army on exterior lines, while Lee, with a short interior line, can concentrate his entire force." Lee, he predicted, would respond to the detachment of a large force from the Army of the Potomac south by utilizing his interior lines to "make another invasion of Maryland and Pennsylvania." The suggestion that the Federal army attempt anything that resembled McClellan's Peninsula Campaign evidently so disturbed Halleck that he was unable or unwilling to grasp Grant's point that a force of 60,000 men in North Carolina would cripple Lee's logistics and render him incapable of conducting a major operation north of the Potomac.[5]

Halleck's rebuke clearly impressed upon Grant the fact that, in his effort to figure out how to crack the Virginia nut, he would have to accommodate the administration's entrenched military prejudices. Consequently, though well aware of the poor prospects for operations against Lee north of Richmond, Grant decided the Army of the Potomac must operate along the overland route. "Lee's army," he instructed Meade, "will be your objective point. Wherever Lee goes, there you will go also."[6]

Fortunately, the option of making a major effort against the Confederates using the James River—the advantages of which Grant's military acumen led him to grasp just as keenly as McClellan and Meade did—was not completely closed to Grant in 1864. Of course, with a presidential contest looming in which McClellan was being touted as the leading Democratic challenger to Lincoln, there was no chance the president would let Grant send the Army of the Potomac to the Peninsula. Yet the fact that Lincoln badly desired the support of War Democrats in November meant that leading War Democrat Benjamin Butler could no longer be denied his desire for an important command engaged in active operations. And at the beginning of 1864, Butler just happened to be in charge of the forces located at Fort Monroe at the tip of the York-James peninsula.

If Butler's command could be increased to a respectable size and maneuvered with any degree of skill, Grant immediately recognized, the Union had the chance to quickly accomplish something big in 1864. Thus he ordered reinforcements from South Carolina to Butler to give him an "Army of the James" of two full army corps. Although at first impressed by Butler, Grant decided to hedge his bets by assigning Baldy Smith to command one of the corps and, as his service under McClellan had made him already well versed in the problems and potential opportunities associated with operations along the James, to advise Butler as necessary. The Army of the James, Grant instructed, would "seize City Point," where the Appomattox and James Rivers converged, and as McClellan had planned to do in July 1862 before the Army of the Potomac was withdrawn from the Peninsula, "operate against Richmond from the south side of the river."[7]

North of Richmond, Grant would have under his personal direction four corps: the Army of the Potomac's Second, Fifth, and Sixth Corps and Ambrose Burnside's Ninth Corps, which, because Burnside still outranked Meade, would be treated as a unit independent from the Army of the Potomac. This force would cross the Rapidan River and try, in Meade's words, "to turn well the enemy's right flank to avoid the intrenchments of Mine Run."[8] If this failed to create the conditions for a decisive victory in battle (and Grant possessed a realistic enough appreciation of military realities not to expect too much), it would at least have two positive results. First, it would keep Lee occupied and prevent him from detaching forces to Richmond to deal with Butler. Hopefully, that would be enough to give Butler a clear shot at Richmond. Second, it would move the Army of the Potomac in such a way that would compel detachment from the Orange and Alexandria and bring it closer to the much more logistically secure and operationally favorable Virginia tidewater.

If things did not work out as planned, Grant would at least have the two armies in a position from which they would be able to link up and operate against Richmond and Lee with the James River as a base. That Grant, like Meade, believed the James was the line to victory in Virginia was evident in a conversation the general in chief had with one of his staff officers on May 3. After directing his aide's attention to a map of Virginia, Grant "with a sweep of his forefinger indicated a line around Richmond and Petersburg, and remarked: 'When my troops are there, Richmond is mine.'" Little wonder that Meade would, after over a month of close interaction with Grant, tell his wife, "he . . . agrees so well with me in his views, I cannot but be rejoiced at his arrival."[9]

Meade's enthusiasm was tempered, however, by recognition that the general in chief's decision to accompany the Army of the Potomac would inevitably cause "the press, and perhaps the public to lose sight of me." He also understood that Grant would exercise a great deal of control over the movements of the Army of the Potomac, and even if his actions corresponded with Meade's own long-held views, "should success attend its operations . . . , my share of the credit will be less." Meade, however, at least found this preferable to his prior situation, when he was held accountable for results without having control over the means for achieving those results, a handicap Grant would surely not have. "My duty is plain," he announced, "to continue quietly to discharge my duties, heartily co-operating with him and under him." In the end he expected that Grant at least would "give me full credit for anything I may do, and if I don't deserve any, I don't desire it."[10]

On May 4 the Army of the Potomac broke camp and moved toward the Rapidan River crossings. Three corps, Warren's Fifth, Sedgwick's Sixth, and Burnside's Ninth, were directed toward Germanna Ford, while Hancock's Second Corps crossed six miles downriver at Ely's Ford. From his commanding observation post on Clark's Mountain and scouts posted along the rivers, Lee was able to quickly deduce the direction of the Federal movements. He ordered his army to break camp and move east along the Orange Turnpike and Orange Plank Road in order to intercept the Federal march and compel Grant to fight in the Wilderness, where the Union advantage in man-power and artillery would be partially negated.

It did not take long for Meade, who had crossed the Rapidan River at midmorning on the fourth, to pick up evidence of Lee's movements. At approximately 7:00 A.M. on the fifth, Meade established his headquarters at Old Wilderness Tavern at the intersection of Germanna Plank Road and the Orange Turnpike. Warren's corps, which had led the Federal march across the Rapidan, had already pushed west on the Orange Turnpike to establish a screen between Lee and the rest of the Army of the Potomac. Shortly after Meade set up headquarters, word arrived from Warren, "the enemy have appeared in force on the Orange pike and are now reported forming line of battle."[11]

Somewhat surprised that the Confederates were able to respond so quickly, Meade mounted his horse and rode west along the turnpike to check on the situation. After Warren confirmed the reports of large enemy forces moving in their direction, Meade remarked, "If there is to be any fighting this side of Mine Run, let us do it right off." Grant immediately agreed: "If any opportunity presents itself for pitching into a part of Lee's army, do so."[12]

As Warren's lead division moved west along the turnpike and into Saunders Field in a futile attempt to drive off Lt. Gen. Richard Ewell's corps, Meade and Grant worked to concentrate the rest of their forces. Sedgwick's corps, which had followed Warren across the Rapidan, was instructed to move into position to the right of the Fifth Corps in support. Hancock was ordered to continue his movements from Chancellorsville, where his corps had bivouacked the night of May 4–5, to Todd's Tavern. Then, once at the latter place, he would move north to secure the point where the Brock and Orange Plank Roads intersected. Burnside's Ninth Corps was ordered to make a forced march and move into a position where it could fill the gap between Warren's left and Hancock's right.

By midafternoon on the fifth, however, Hancock was still far from the critical Brock Road–Orange Plank Road intersection. If the Confederates could seize that point, they would drive a

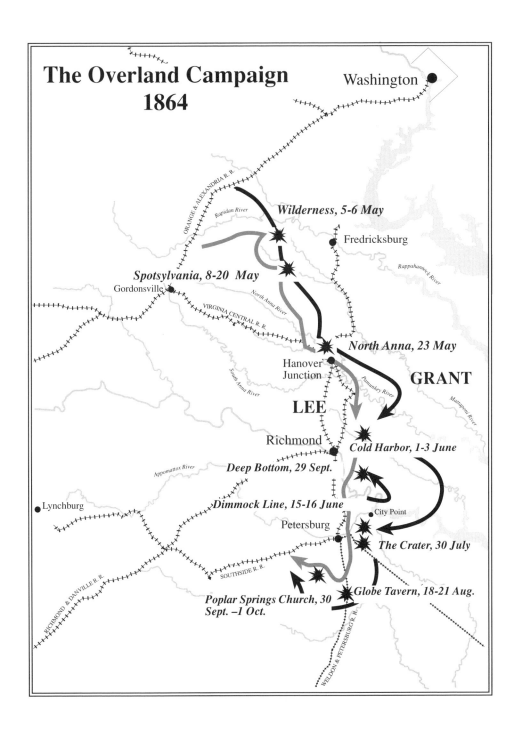

The Overland Campaign
1864

Washington

ORANGE & ALEXANDRIA R. R.

Rapidan River

Wilderness, 5-6 May

Fredericksburg

Rappahannock River

Spotsylvania, 8-20 May

Gordonsville

VIRGINIA CENTRAL R. R.

North Anna River

North Anna, 23 May

Hanover
Junction

South Anna River

Pamunkey River

GRANT

Mattaponi River

LEE

Richmond

Cold Harbor, 1-3 June

Appomattox River

Deep Bottom, 29 Sept.

Lynchburg

Dimmock Line, 15-16 June

City Point

Petersburg

The Crater, 30 July

SOUTHSIDE R. R.

*Poplar Springs Church, 30
Sept. –1 Oct.*

Globe Tavern, 18-21 Aug.

RICHMOND & DANVILLE R. R.

WELDON & PETERSBURG R. R.

wedge between Hancock and the rest of Grant's forces. To prevent this from happening, Meade ordered Brig. Gen. George Getty to take his division of Sedgwick's corps as quickly as he could to the intersection and "hold this crossing at all hazards until the arrival of the Second Corps."[13] Thanks to Meade's quick action, Getty arrived just in time to fight off Lt. Gen. A.P. Hill's corps as it advanced from the west along Orange Plank Road. When Hancock finally arrived, the Federals counterattacked and drove Hill's command back in some disarray before nightfall.

The next morning Hancock opened the fighting by launching a sledgehammer attack along the Orange Plank Road that overwhelmed Hill's men. "Tell General Meade," Hancock shouted to a courier from headquarters, "we are driving them most beautifully."[14] When the Confederates reached a clearing around the Widow Tapp Farm, however, Lee personally rallied Hill's men. Longstreet's corps then arrived on the battlefield and took advantage of an unfinished-railroad cut to smash Hancock's left. The Federals managed to rally behind breastworks and, in a brutal fight that took place amid a horrific forest fire, held on to the position along Brock Road until nightfall.

It had been a terrible fight, but Grant believed the battle "was decidedly in our favor" and was determined to keep moving south toward the James. At 6:30 A.M. on May 7, he instructed Meade, "Make all preparations during the day for a night march to take position at Spotsylvania Court House with one army corps." The general immediately agreed with Grant's decision—after all, it was not much different from his own plan the previous fall to move in the direction of Fredericksburg before and after Mine Run. Meade assigned Warren's corps, which had not been heavily engaged on May 6, the task of seizing Spotsylvania. Warren would march south to Spotsylvania along Brock Road while Hancock's shifted south to Todd's Tavern and Sedgwick, followed by Burnside, moved to Chancellorsville. Sedgwick would then turn south and march to Spotsylvania to support Warren. Grant's objective was "to get between [Lee's] army and Richmond if possible; and, if not, to draw him into the open field."[15]

Unfortunately, Lee was able to successfully react to this move and get a strong force in position on Laurel Hill, which dominated the road to Spotsylvania, in time to block the Federals. Assaults by Warren's and Sedgwick's corps on May 8 and 9 failed to dislodge the Confederates. Furious at the failure to win the race to Spotsylvania, Meade directed his wrath at Maj. Gen. Phillip Sheridan, whom Grant had brought with him from the West and installed as commander of the Army of the Potomac's cavalry. Had Sheridan's cavalry not clogged the road, Meade believed, Warren's corps might have been able to reach Laurel Hill in time to deny it to the Rebels. For his part, Sheridan was angry at Meade for personally directing the movements of the cavalry. During a heated exchange on May 8, Sheridan exclaimed that he was tired of Meade's interference with his command and that "I could whip Stuart if he (Meade) would only let me."[16]

Meade went to Grant's headquarters to discuss the situation and described his confrontation with Sheridan. When Meade related Sheridan's boast that he could whip Stuart, instead of sustaining Meade, Grant decided to gratify his cavalry commander's wish for independence. "Did Sheridan say that?" Grant asked Meade on hearing of his boast. "Well, he generally knows what he is talking about. Let him start right out and do it."[17] Although no doubt stung by this turn of events, Meade immediately complied with Grant's wishes and issued orders to Sheridan, instructing him to concentrate the army's cavalry and undertake a raid toward the James River with the objective of bringing the Rebel cavalry to battle.

As Sheridan headed off on his raid, Meade and Grant battled Lee at Spotsylvania. The Union effort got off to a bad start, with the Confederates easily repulsing a series of attacks against Laurel Hill and frustrating a Federal attempt to cross the Po River to turn their position on May 9–10. To make matters worse, Sedgwick was killed while examining his lines on May 9, which placed an untried Horatio Wright in command of the Sixth Corps. A bold, twelve-regiment assault under Col. Emory Upton on May 10 managed to achieve an all-too-brief penetration of the Rebel position, however. This inspired Grant

PHILIP HENRY SHERIDAN

Born New York 1831; Sheridan's date and place of birth remain matters of speculation; Sheridan himself gave conflicting information; he may have been born in Ireland or aboard ship during his Irish parents' passage to the United

States; whatever the case, the family moved to Ohio when Sheridan was still an infant; he entered the U.S. Military Academy with the class of 1852, but disciplinary problems delayed his graduation by a year; he finished thirty-fourth in the 1853 class of fifty-two that included John Bell Hood, James B. McPherson, and John M. Schofield; after years of service on the frontier with the 4th Infantry, Sheridan was still a 2d lieutenant on the eve of the Civil War; promoted to 1st lieutenant in March 1861 and captain, 13th Infantry, in May, he served as chief quartermaster and commissary for the Army of Southwest Missouri and was detailed to General Henry Halleck's headquarters during the advance on Corinth, Mississippi; in May 1862 he entered the volunteer army as colonel of the 2d Michigan Cavalry and, by July, was promoted to brigadier general, U.S. Volunteers; he commanded an infantry division at Perryville and Stone's River, gaining promotion to

major general, U.S. Volunteers, to date from December 1862; Sheridan's division was routed at Chickamauga in September 1863, but spearheaded the unauthorized assault that drove the Confederates from Missionary Ridge in November; when General Ulysses S. Grant was named overall commander of Union forces and went east to face General Robert E. Lee, he selected Sheridan to lead the Army of the Potomac's Cavalry Corps; throughout the spring and early summer of 1864, Sheridan's troopers duelled with the once-supreme Rebel cavalry with mixed results; he was victorious in the clash at Yellow Tavern, in which Confederate cavalry commander J.E.B. Stuart was mortally wounded; in response to Confederate General Jubal Early's move on Washington, Grant created the Middle Military Division and placed Sheridan in command; Sheridan's Army of the Shenandoah, consisting of two infantry corps and three large divisions of cavalry, defeated Early at Winchester and Fisher's Hill but narrowly escaped disaster at Cedar Creek when the Rebels surprised Sheridan's army during his absence; Sheridan's ride from Winchester to Cedar Creek to rally his men is among the most well-publicized events of the war; during the fall and winter of 1864-1865, in an awesome display of total war, Sheridan's troops laid waste to the Shenandoah Valley, depriving Lee of much-needed supplies and incurring the wrath of Southerners for generations to come; the fiery Sheridan became a national hero; having been promoted to brigadier general in the regular army in September 1864, he became major general in November; in the spring of 1865 Sheridan, with the bulk of his command, rejoined Grant on the Petersburg front and played a pivotal role in the closing stages of the war; given wide discretion, Sheridan's cavalry ran roughshod over the Rebels at Five Forks and Sayler's Creek, finally cornering Lee's army near Appomattox; while extremely successful on the battlefield, Sheridan's abrasive manner and quick temper led to the unfair removal of General G.K. Warren, a controversy that raged for years; immediately after Lee's surrender, Sheridan was dispatched to the south Texas border with Mexico to discourage French intentions in that country; thereafter his heavy-handed conduct as the reconstruction commander of the Fifth Military District (Texas and Louisiana) brought his removal; when Grant became president and William T. Sherman filled his spot as commanding general, Sheridan became lieutenant general; as commander of the Military Division of the Missouri, he was an aggressive prosecutor of the Indian Wars; during this period he was also an official observer of the Franco-Prussian War and supported the creation of Yellowstone National Park; in 1884, on the retirement of Sherman, Sheridan became commanding general; in June 1888 he was awarded his fourth star; General Sheridan died shortly thereafter at Nonquitt, Massachusetts. He remains among the most influential soldiers in the nation's history.

to plan a massive assault on the "Mule Shoe," a bulge in the center of Lee's defensive line, first thing on May 12. Like Upton's attack, this too managed to achieve some initial success, but despite taking over three thousand prisoners, it ultimately failed to achieve decisive results.

In the week that followed, Grant, with Meade serving as a mere conduit for orders, maneuvered units back and forth in an attempt to find a weak point in the Confederate position. After fighting at the Mule Shoe ended early on the morning of May 13, Warren and Wright moved behind and around Hancock's and Burnside's positions in an attempt to turn the Rebel right. Constant heavy rains, however, frustrated this

ROBERT E. LEE

Born Virginia 1807; son of Ann Hill (Carter) Lee and Henry "Light-Horse Harry" Lee, who died when Robert was eleven; received early education in Alexandria, Virginia, schools; graduated second in his class at U.S. Military Academy in 1829, without receiving a demerit in four years; appointed 2d lieutenant of engineers in 1829, 1st lieutenant in 1836, and captain in 1838; served at Fort Pulaski, Fort Monroe, Fort Hamilton, and superintended engineering project for St. Louis harbor; married Mary Ann Randolph Custis, whose father's estate of "Arlington" on the Virginia shore of the Potomac opposite Washington became Lee's home in 1857 after the death of his father-in-law; in 1846 Lee, then a captain, joined General Winfield Scott's Vera Cruz expedition and invasion of Mexico; Lee's extraordinary industry and capacity won him a brilliant reputation and the lasting confidence and esteem of Scott; wounded in 1847, Lee won three brevet promotions to major, lieutenant colonel, and colonel for gallant and meritorious conduct in the battles of Cerro Gordo, Contreras, Churubusco, and Chapultepec; served as superintendent of the U.S. Military

movement, and Lee easily countered it. Then Wright and Humphreys suggested to Grant that "a return by night to the enemy's left" at the Mule Shoe, "which would probably be abandoned, or very much weakened by our concentration on his right might afford a good opportunity to attack there."[18] Grant agreed, and on May 18 Hancock's corps and part of Wright's made another assault on the Confederate trenches but found the enemy were more than ready for them; the Federals never even reached the Confederate works.

Over a week of fighting at Spotsylvania produced little more than horrific butchery and frustration for the Federals. To be sure, the operations around Spotsylvania produced a rate of

Academy from 1852 to 1855; promoted to lieutenant colonel 2d Cavalry in 1855; commanded Marines sent to Harpers Ferry to capture John Brown after his raid; promoted to colonel 1st Cavalry in 1861; having refused command of Federal armies, his first Confederate command led to failure at Cheat Mountain in western Virginia; after serving along the South Atlantic coast, he returned to Virginia as military advisor to President Jefferson Davis until June 1862 when he replaced the wounded Joseph E. Johnston in command of forces that became known as the Army of Northern Virginia; for nearly three years, Lee's aggressive campaigns and effective defenses frustrated Union efforts to capture the Confederate capital; not until February 1865—two months before his surrender—did he become over-all commander of Confederate forces; after the war, he accepted the presidency of Washington College (later changed to Washington and Lee University) in Lexington, Virginia, where he remained until his death in 1870. Theodore Roosevelt proclaimed Lee "without exception the very greatest of all the great captains." "Lee possessed every virtue of other great commanders without their vices," announced an orator. "He was a foe without hate; a friend without treachery; a victor without oppression, and a victim without murmuring. He was a public officer without vices; a private citizen without reproach; a Christian without hypocrisy and a man without guile." Bold, modest, and heroic, Lee once confessed that if war were less terrible he would become too fond of it. His greatest biographer characterized him as "a simple gentleman."

attrition favorable to the Federals, but Grant, like Meade, had little taste for such an approach and much preferred a strategy of maneuvering for position. Thus, when he finally concluded that nothing decisive could be accomplished at Spotsylvania, he instructed Meade to make preparations for yet another move by the left flank. "Even Grant," Meade informed his wife on May 19, "thought it useless to knock our heads against a brick wall."[19]

Lee, however, managed to frustrate the Federal maneuver by falling behind the North Anna River and establishing a strong position there. After three days of fighting demonstrated that nothing could be accomplished at the North Anna, on May 26 Grant decided to once again try to move around Lee's right. He ordered Meade to send the Army of the Potomac across the Pamunkey River at Hanovertown. Crossing the Pamunkey put the Army of the Potomac back on the Peninsula, "the scene," wrote one man, "of McClellan's campaign of two years before. We couldn't help thinking how McClellan had got the army almost to Richmond with hardly the loss of a man, while Grant had lost already thousands more than we cared to guess."[20]

After crossing the river and pushing forward to Totopotomoy Creek, however, Grant and Meade found Lee in a strong defensive line. The two sides skirmished for a few days, with the most significant action occurring on May 30, when Lee unsuccessfully attacked Warren's corps near Bethesda Church. Finally, unable to find a weak spot in the enemy's defenses, Grant decided to shift his forces south and extend his left in the direction of a crossroads known as Cold Harbor. Less than five miles from there was Gaines's Mill, where Meade had first led men in combat two years earlier.

During the Army of the Potomac's operations from Spotsylvania to the Pamunkey River, the Grant-Meade relationship experienced a number of twists and turns. First, at Spotsylvania, several members of Grant's staff began thinking that things might go more smoothly if their boss ignored Meade altogether. When Grant got wind of their discussions, he immediately moved to stop any talk of Meade's displacement. "Meade and I," he informed his staff, "are in close contact in the field; he is capable and perfectly subordinate, and by attending to the details he relieves me of much unnecessary work, and gives me more time to mature my general plans." Indeed, he even saw fit to send a telegram to Washington stating that Meade had "more than met my most sanguine expectations" and recommended both him and Sherman for promotion to major general in the regular army.[21]

Nonetheless, during the operations around Spotsylvania, Grant did, in fact, command the Army of the Potomac and determine the movements of its corps. Meade's role was simply to serve as Grant's leading advisor and translate the commanding general's wishes into orders for the army, tasks he performed to Grant's satisfaction but found frustrating personally. Meade tried to salve his ego by telling himself and his wife that a newspaper article stating the Army of the Potomac was "directed by Grant, commanded by Meade, and led by Hancock, Sedgwick, and Warren" made "a quite good distinction and about hits the nail on the head." But as the armies marched south from Spotsylvania, he acknowledged, "from the very nature of things, Grant had taken the control."[22]

Not surprisingly, Meade privately began to complain about what he considered "a very unjust" position. Further fouling his mood was the decision of Assistant Secretary of War Charles Dana, a Radical Republican who was accompanying the Army of the Potomac and possessed a deep antipathy toward its high command, to take a poke at that army and its commanders. After making sure Meade and Grant were in attendance at headquarters on May 24, Dana gleefully read aloud a letter from Sherman. In it the general expressed faith in the Union effort in Virginia if Grant could only "sustain the confidence, the esprit, and the pluck of his army and impress the Virginians with the knowledge that the Yankees can and will fight them fair and square. . . . Out here the enemy knows we can and will fight like the devil." Meade immediately responded: "Sir! I consider that dispatch an insult to the army I command and to me personally. The Army of the Potomac does not require General Grant's inspiration or anybody else's inspiration to make it fight!"[23]

After this incident, Grant began to loosen his grip on the Army of the Potomac, though only in part to accommodate Meade's bruised ego. More importantly, events elsewhere in Virginia demonstrated to Grant that he needed to pull back from tactical supervision of only one of the armies under his command as general in chief. In mid-May Maj. Gen. Franz Sigel's incompetence led a Union army to defeat in the Shenandoah Valley at New Market, and Benjamin Butler, after successfully reaching City Point, let a small Confederate force pen his Army of the James between the James and Appomattox Rivers "as if . . . in a bottle strongly corked."[24] Butler's failure dashed whatever hopes Grant had for the success of his plan for quick victory in Virginia. Together, Butler's and Sigel's failures impressed upon him the fact that that he could not simultaneously exercise direct command over the Army of the Potomac and keep a proper eye on the rest of the Union war effort.

Consequently, in late May and early June, Grant made a number of significant decisions indicating a determination to turn over more of the army's tactical leadership to Meade. First, on May 24 he issued instructions terminating his practice of treating the Ninth Corps as an independent unit. Regardless of seniority, Burnside was going to take orders from Meade. Second, when Baldy Smith's corps of Butler's army was ordered to the Army of the Potomac on May 26, Grant explicitly directed that it would be treated as a subordinate unit and subject to Meade's orders. Finally, he left responsibility for tactical management of the Battle of Cold Harbor on June 3 to Meade.

The decision to launch the disastrous attack at Cold Harbor was Grant's alone, however. Although on May 29 Meade had stated "we will continue to manoeuvre till we compel Lee to retire into the defense of Richmond," there is no evidence that he disagreed with the decision to assault Lee's position. Indeed, even after the first moments of the attack on the morning of June 3 demonstrated that the Rebels held an impregnable position, Meade remained uncharacteristically aggressive. With the incident with Dana at headquarters no doubt still on his mind, he seized on whatever feeble signs of progress were reported as a pretense for continuing to press the attack all along the line well after the front-line commanders had given up hope. Not until an hour after Grant wrote him at 12:30 P.M. authorizing an end to the attack ("The opinion of corps commanders not being sanguine of success . . . , you may direct a suspension of farther advance") did Meade finally issue orders ending the futile Federal assaults.[25]

Although the fighting at Cold Harbor reflected no credit on either Meade or Grant, the former did take comfort afterward that the fighting there, and the Overland Campaign as a whole, had provided "the clearest indications I could wish of my sound judgment, both at Williamsport and Mine Run." He wrote his wife: "In every instance that we have attacked the enemy in an entrenched position, we have failed. . . . So, likewise, whenever the enemy has attacked us in position, he has been repulsed." No doubt with Sherman's words still burning in his consciousness, Meade continued: "I think Grant has had his eyes opened, and is willing to admit now that Virginia and Lee's army is not Tennessee and Bragg's army. Whether the people will ever realize this fact remains to be seen."[26]

7
PETERSBURG

After the setback on June 3, Grant found himself at an operational crossroads. He clearly could not remain at Cold Harbor. To do so after the failed Union assaults would foster an impression in the North that the Rebels had checked his grand offensive, and with a presidential election only months away, that was politically unacceptable. Alternately, he could break from his established pattern and move to the north and west in an attempt to get around Lee's left and operate against Richmond from the north. That surely would please General Halleck (and by extension President Lincoln), who had become greatly distressed at Grant's continual movements to the south and east toward the James River. Halleck's anxiety became particularly acute when Grant sent word of his intention, after crossing the North Anna River, to shift his supply base to White House on the Pamunkey River—which had last been used for that purpose by McClellan in 1862. To anyone who would listen, Halleck began letting them know that he believed Grant should move back to the north and operate against Richmond from that direction, using the rail-roads as his supply line.

Finally, although aware that Washington strategists might howl at such a suggestion, Grant could carry out his long-standing wish to get the Army of the Potomac to the James River by again moving to the left. Even before the debacle at Cold Harbor, Meade correctly anticipated Grant would do this. In late May and early June 1864, he approvingly predicted Grant would "repeat this turning operation . . . till Lee gets into Richmond. . . . Then will begin the tedious process of a quasi-siege, like that of Sebastopol."[1]

When Grant issued orders for the army to move to the James, with an eye on crossing to its south side and operating on Petersburg—which was McClellan's intention before the administration ordered the withdrawal from Harrison's Landing in August 1862—Meade was delighted. "To-day we commence a flank march," he informed his wife, "to unite with Butler on the James. If it is successful, as I think it will be, it will bring us the last act of the Richmond drama, which I trust will have but few scenes in it, and will end fortunately and vic-toriously for us." On the other side of the trenches, Lee had reached a similar conclusion. Before Cold Harbor, he had told one of his subordinates: "We must destroy this army of Grant's before he gets to [the] James River. If he gets there, it will become a siege, and then it will be a mere question of time."[2]

The march to and the crossing of the James River were almost flawlessly executed. The Federal deception plans suc-cessfully fooled Lee and prevented him from doing anything to catch the armies on the march. "All goes on like a miracle," wrote one astonished observer, "Lee appears to have had no idea of our crossing the James River." "We are now on the nat-ural road to Richmond," one officer proclaimed upon reaching the James River, "all is right."[3]

Unfortunately, when the Federals reached the outskirts of lightly defended Petersburg on June 15, Baldy Smith tested the Confederate fortifications with such caution that Lee was able to figure out what was going on and begin rushing forces southward. Anxious that the fruits of his march might be lost

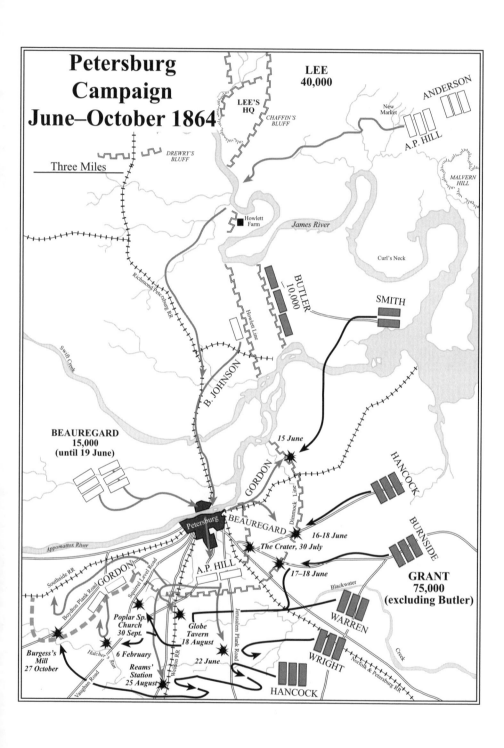

Petersburg
Campaign
June–October 1864

without effective leadership at the front, early on the morning of the sixteenth, Grant ordered Meade to Petersburg to take charge of the situation "and, if practicable, push the enemy across the Appomattox."[4]

Despite Smith's failure the previous day, when he arrived on the scene at 2:00 P.M. and assumed command, Meade shared Grant's belief that a determined push could take Petersburg. Unfortunately for Grant and Meade, the Army of the Potomac was beginning to show the effects of the month of grisly work that had commenced in the Wilderness. Corps commanders were physically and mentally spent, constant fighting had worn down the army's ranks, and those who remained at their posts had reached the limits of their endurance and were extremely reluctant to assault any entrenched positions. In contrast, Meade was, wrote one of Grant's staff officers, "the personification of earnest vigorous action. . . . He sent rousing dispatches to all points of the line, and paced up and down upon the field as he watched the progress of the operations . . . , and if he was severe in his reprimands and showed faults of temper, he certainly displayed no faults as a commander."[5]

Despite Meade's best efforts, the Federal offensive against Petersburg on June 16–18 lacked the dash that had distinguished earlier attacks and failed to break the Confederates defenses. "I cannot say that our men went in well, or at all as if they meant to carry the works," wrote one witness afterward. "I trust it will be the last attempt at this most absurd way of attacking entrenchments. . . . Even the stupidest private now knows it cannot succeed, and the natural consequence follows: the men will not try it. The very sight of a bank of fresh earth now brings them to a dead halt." One of Meade's staff officers lamented: "The men went in, but not with spirit. General Meade was disappointed, but . . . you cannot strike a full blow with a wounded hand."[6]

With the failure of the attacks, Grant directed Meade to commence siege operations south of the James against Petersburg; Butler's Army of the James did the same against Richmond north of the river. Both Grant and Meade hoped, however, that lengthy operations could be avoided. Their attention was particularly attracted to the extensive system of rail lines for which Petersburg was a hub. If the Army of the Potomac could extend its lines to the west and seize control of the Weldon and the Southside Railroads, it would cripple Lee's army and make it impossible for it to sustain a lengthy defense. Consequently, on June 20 Meade, with Grant's approval, decided to push the Second and Sixth Corps west, seize the two lines, "and endeavor to stretch to the Appomattox."[7]

The next day both corps crossed Jerusalem Plank Road and attempted to push to the Weldon Railroad. Lee, however, quickly realized what the Federals were doing and rushed two divisions to the scene, which viscously counterattacked and nearly pushed the Federals back to Jerusalem Plank Road. Despite the failure of this first strike at the railroads, Grant and Meade remained convinced of the soundness of their strategy. The Army of the Potomac would spend the next month consolidating their new position and constructing a series of forts and redoubts south of the Appomattox connecting their lines from the river to just west of the Jerusalem Plank Road. The generals intended to make their line strong enough so that only one or two corps could hold it and they could use the rest of the Army of the Potomac for operations against the Weldon and Southside Railroads.

The next Petersburg offensive, however, would be of a different and decidedly unique character. One of the regiments in Ambrose Burnside's corps was composed of men from the Pennsylvania coal mines, one of whom conceived a plan to dig a mine underneath the Confederate trenches, fill it with gunpowder, and then set it off, blowing a hole in the Rebel line big enough to permit a successful assault. Burnside loved the idea; Meade did not. Grant, however, was well aware that Washington would have little patience for a long, drawn-out operation at Petersburg. Moreover, with the Sixth Corps having been ordered to the capital in response to Union defeats in the Shenandoah Valley, Grant knew it would be several weeks before he could make another push for the railroads. He told Meade to let Burnside dig his mine.

By the last week of July 1864, Burnside was ready to carry out his plan. After the mine exploded, he intended to exploit the breakthrough by pushing forward Brig. Gen. Edward Ferrero's fresh division of African American troops, which had been receiving special training for the task. On July 28, however, two days before the planned assault, Meade told Burnside: "I cannot approve of your placing the negro troops in the advance. . . . I do not think they should be called upon to do as important a work as that which you propose to do, certainly not called upon to lead." He further protested, wrote one observer, "that they were a new division and had never been under fire, while this was an operation requiring the very best troops."[8] There was more to it than this, though. Meade had yet to see African American troops do anything that would induce him to set aside his doubts regarding their ability to fight as well as white soldiers, which had been manifest in his making a point throughout the Overland Campaign of keeping Ferrero's division in the rear, guarding supply trains, and thus well away from the fighting.

Burnside objected to this decision so vehemently that Meade decided to bring the matter to Grant's attention. Unlike with Sheridan at Spotsylvania, this time Grant sustained Meade. Burnside then turned the matter over to his other division commanders, who drew straws to decide who would take Ferrero's place in the attack. Unfortunately, the man who drew the fateful straw was Brig. Gen. James Ledlie, perhaps the least competent division commander in the entire Union army.

On July 29 Meade issued his orders for the attack. Once the mine was sprung, Meade directed that Burnside's "assaulting columns will immediately move upon the breach, seize the crest [of Cemetery Hill just behind the Confederate line], and effect a lodging there." Warren's Fifth Corps and Maj. Gen. E.O.C. Ord's Eighteenth Corps, the latter having just arrived from Louisiana, would support the flanks of the assaulting columns and then follow up the Ninth Corps's success. That night Meade met with Burnside and the commanders of his three white divisions to make sure they understood what was

EDWARD O.C. ORD

Born Maryland 1818; appointed to U.S. Military Academy at age sixteen, graduated seventeenth out of thirty-one cadets in 1839; brevetted 2d lieutenant in 3rd Artillery; served in Second Seminole War, promoted to 1st lieutenant for his service there; during the Mexican War stationed in California; served at numerous frontier posts; in 1859 he was at the artillery school at Fort Monroe, Virginia during John Brown's raid on Harper's Ferry and participated in the expedition that captured Brown; was captain of the 3rd Artillery when war broke out; in September 1861 promoted to brigadier general of volunteers; given command of a brigade in George McCall's division of "Pennsylvania Reserves," saw his first action at Dranesville in December 1861; transferred to divisional command in Irwin McDowell's corps and on May 3, 1862, was promoted to major general and reassigned to the Western Theater; participated in the Corinth campaign and was severely wounded in action near Pocahontas, Mississippi; returned to duty during the siege of Vicksburg in June 1863 as commander of XIII Corps; led his corps through the Jackson Campaign; in spring of 1864 returned to the Eastern Theater; given command of VIII Corps during the siege of Petersburg; soon after was transferred command of the XVIII Corps; led an assault on Fort Harrison in September 1864 and was seriously wounded; he recovered and in January 1865 replaced Benjamin Butler as commander of the Army of the James and Department of North Carolina; he remained in this position until the surrender at Appomattox; after the war Ord remained in the army, retiring as a major general in 1881; in 1883 while on a trip to Vera Cruz he contracted yellow fever and died in Havana on July 22; he is buried in Arlington National Cemetery.

GOUVERNEUR K. WARREN

Born New York 1830; graduated from the U.S. Military Academy second in his class in 1850; brevet 2d lieutenant Topographical Engineers; promoted to 2d lieutenant in 1854 and to 1st lieutenant in 1856. Before the Civil War, he surveyed the Mississippi River Delta, supervised river and canal improvements, compiled maps and reports of the Pacific Railroad exploration, served as chief engineer of the Sioux Expedition where he fought Indians and made

maps in Dakota and Nebraska territories; taught mathematics at West Point. In 1861 appointed lieutenant colonel 5th New York Volunteer Infantry, he saw action at Big Bethel and was then promoted to colonel of his regiment and to captain of topographical engineers; in 1862 participated in the Peninsular Campaign and the Battle of the Seven Days, where he was wounded at Gaines' Mill and brevetted lieutenant colonel, U.S. Army, for gallantry; served in the battles of Second Bull Run, Antietam, Fredericksburg, and Chancellorsville; promoted to brigadier general, U.S. Volunteers; in 1863 promoted to major general, U.S. Volunteers, and transferred to regular army engineers; named chief engineer for the Army of the Potomac and married Emily Forbes Chase of Baltimore, with whom he had a son and a daughter; wounded at Gettysburg, where he distinguished himself at Little Round Top and received a brevet promotion to colonel, U.S. Army, for his gallant conduct; commanding the Second Corps from August 1863 to March 1864, he participated in a number of engagements, notably that at Bristoe Station, for which he was brevetted brigadier general and later major general, U.S. Army. Warren commanded the Fifth Corps in actions from the Wilderness to Five Forks, where General Philip H. Sheridan, with Grant's approval, removed him from command for alleged slowness in carrying out orders; Warren resigned from the volunteer service in 1865, but remained in the regular army as major until his promotion to lieutenant colonel engineers in 1879; after repeated requests, fourteen years after the war, he received a court of inquiry that exonerated him of Sheridan's charges. His career shattered by these charges, Warren "died of a broken heart" at Newport, Rhode Island, in 1882.

expected of them. "Immediate advantage," he emphasized, "must be taken of the confusion of the enemy caused by the explosion of the mine to gain the crest." If they were unsuccessful in gaining the crest immediately, Meade told his subordinates he did not believe they would achieve their objective, in which case "the troops must be withdrawn at once" to the protection of their trenches.[9]

Early on the morning of July 30, Meade met up with Grant to watch Burnside's assault. To Meade's surprise, the mine worked spectacularly and blew a gaping hole in the enemy lines. When he learned that the attacking forces had an open road to Petersburg in front of them, Meade immediately fired off a telegram to Burnside: "Prisoners taken say there is no line in their rear. . . . Our chance is now; push your men forward at all hazards (white and black), and don't lose time in making formations, but rush for the crest."[10] Burnside's men did their best but, due to the incompetence of Ledlie and the other division commanders, lacked the leadership and direction necessary to push through the Crater with sufficient vigor to seize Cemetery Hill. This allowed the Confederates to rush reinforcements to the scene, successfully restore their lines, and inflict horrific casualties on the Federals.

Meade watched the debacle unfold with cold fury. Then, as the survivors fell back to their original lines, he rode over to Ninth Corps headquarters and got into a argument with Burnside that one witness described as "decidedly peppery, and went far toward confirming one's belief in the wealth and flexibility of the English language as a medium of personal dispute."[11] Two weeks later Burnside was granted a leave of absence from the army and turned command of the Ninth Corps over to Maj. Gen. John G. Parke.

At Burnside's request, Grant then authorized a court of inquiry to investigate the Crater fiasco. Chaired by Winfield Scott Hancock and composed of other officers friendly to Meade, it began taking testimony on August 6. Meade appeared before the court four days later. A rigorous cross-examination by Burnside's lawyer failed to shake Meade's belief that the failure was a result of poor leadership in the

JOHN G. PARKE

Born Pennsylvania 1827; graduated U.S. Military Academy 1849, second in a class of forty-three; commissioned 2d Lieutenant in the Corps of Topographical Engineers; conducted several boundary surveys before the war, including northwest border between U.S. and Canada; commissioned brigadier general of volunteers November 1861; commanded a brigade in General Ambrose Burnside's 1862 North Carolina campaign; promoted major general July 18, 1862; served as Burnside's chief of staff through the Maryland and Fredericksburg Campaigns; after Burnside's removal and assignment as commander of the Department of the Ohio became commander of the IX Corps; in early June 1863 his corps was sent to reinforce General Ulysses S. Grant at Vicksburg, where he participated in the last phases of the siege and the subsequent capture of Jackson; returned to Ohio in late July and was involved in the Knoxville campaign, once again becoming chief of staff when Burnside assumed command of the IX Corps prior to the 1864 Overland Campaign; the IX  Corps was a separate entity apart from the Army of the Potomac and answered directly to Grant by virtue of Burnside's seniority over Meade until May 24, when it was assigned to Meade; after the fiasco at the Battle of the Crater he replaced Burnside as commander of the IX Corps; fought at Peebles's Farm and Hatcher's Run; was temporarily in command of the Army of the Potomac during the attack on Fort Stedman due to Meade's absence; after the war he served as superintendent of the U.S. Military Academy from 1887-1889; and later became president of the Society of the Army of the Potomac; died in 1900 and buried in Philadelphia.

Ninth Corps. Nonetheless, the general wrote his wife that evening, "I feel sorry for Burnside, because I really believe the man half the time don't know what he is about, and is hardly responsible for his acts."[12]

Given the composition of the court, it surprised no one when its report, issued on September 9, placed the blame for the defeat at the Crater squarely on the leadership of Ninth Corps for failing to follow Meade instructions that "columns of assault should be employed."[13] And although Burnside complained bitterly in his testimony of Meade's decision not to let Ferrero's division lead the attack, no mention was made of it in the court's findings or opinion.

The Crater investigation did not, however, compel a suspension of operations against Petersburg. On August 14 Grant and Meade ordered Hancock's corps to conduct an expedition against Confederate defenses north of the James. Lee responded to this move by shifting forces from the Petersburg front, which he did quickly enough to foil Hancock's operations against Deep Bottom. But in doing so, he created a favorable situation for the Federals south of the James, which Meade advised Grant must be seized. With the general in chief's approval, Meade withdrew the Fifth Corps from the trenches and on August 16 directed Warren, supported by the Ninth Corps, to take "advantage of the weakening of the enemy's line south of the Appomattox to effect a lodgment upon the Weldon Railroad."[14]

Warren began his movement on the morning of August 18 and successfully reached the Weldon at Globe Tavern shortly before noon. He then constructed fortifications behind which his command repulsed a series of fierce Confederate counterattacks. When the fighting ended on August 21, the Union had achieved a secure foothold on the Weldon Railroad. Union engineers immediately went to work constructing a chain of forts and redoubts extending the Federal lines from Jerusalem Plank Road to Globe Tavern.

One month later Grant decided the time had come for another offensive. He conceived a plan whereby Butler, north of the James, and Meade, south of the river, would advance against the Confederate defenses, hoping that Lee would be unable to cope with both forces at the same time. Meade identified as his objective Boydton Plank Road, for if he could get a significant force there, he would sever another major Confederate supply line and perhaps even strike for the

Southside Railroad. For the operation, he placed the Fifth Corps and two divisions from the Ninth Corps under the overall command of Warren and ordered them to move forward from the position on the Weldon Railroad that had been seized the previous month.

Although Warren's men failed to reach Boydton Plank Road, they did manage to advance to Poplar Spring Church. Then, against Meade's wishes, upon encountering moderate resistance, Warren immediately halted his advance and began digging trenches. As they had the previous month, these fortifications proved strong enough to enable his men to repulse Confederate attempts on October 1 to drive them back to their previous position. Although disappointed that the "Fifth Petersburg Offensive" did not achieve more, Meade quickly extended his trench line out to Warren's new position.

Despite these accomplishments, the late summer of 1864 was by no means a happy time for Meade. The Burnside investigation, of course, worked out quite well. But Federal set backs in the Shenandoah Valley sparked a series of events that provided Meade with cause for concern regarding the administration's approach to military affairs in general and his case in particular.

After Sigel's defeat at New Market on May 15, Grant had sent Maj. Gen. David Hunter to the Shenandoah Valley to take charge. But after a promising beginning, Hunter made a series of poor decisions that opened the Shenandoah Valley to Confederate forces under Lt. Gen. Jubal Early. Early drove his small army to the gates of Washington itself in early July, and though he was unable to do more than that, the raid provoked much consternation in the capital and compelled Grant to dispatch the Sixth Corps from Petersburg. To Halleck, Early's operations vindicated his belief that a big mistake had been made when Grant was allowed to take the Army of the Potomac south of the James River. Lincoln too was not pleased and decided a personal visit to Grant's headquarters was necessary to impress upon him the fact that, although he was being allowed to operate from the James, more attention needed to be paid to the defense of Washington.

Grant responded by proposing that all the forces in the Valley and around Washington be placed under a single commander. Grant first suggested William B. Franklin for the command. Franklin, however, had made himself anathema to the administration through his enduring loyalty to McClellan and advocacy of returning to the James after the Fredericksburg debacle. Thus Lincoln rejected Franklin. Grant then suggested Meade.

Two days before meeting with the president on July 31, Grant told Meade that he had sent his name to Washington as a possible commander for the forces around the capital. Meade did not respond to the suggestion favorably or unfavorably but merely told Grant he would obey whatever orders he received. In a letter to his wife that night, Meade explained his mixed feelings regarding the matter. "So far as having an independent command, which the Army of the Potomac is not, I would like this change very well; but in other respects, to have to manage Couch, Hunter, Wallace, and Auger," he wrote, "and to be managed by the President, Secretary and Halleck, will be a pretty trying position that no man in his senses could desire. I am quite indifferent how it turns out."[15]

With Meade evidently "indifferent" to the matter, Grant decided to send Sheridan to Washington instead. When he read in the newspapers that Sheridan had been assigned to command the Middle Military Division, Meade experienced a sudden change of heart. The command now appeared to be much more significant than Grant had led Meade to believe. Feeling he had been betrayed, when he encountered the general in chief on August 13, Meade asked him how he could give Sheridan, his junior in rank, such a major independent command. Meade viewed the decision as an insult and "regretted it had not been deemed a simple matter of justice to place me in this independent command."[16] To Meade's immense distress, Grant said nothing in reply, though he later explained that he feared Meade's critics would interpret his reassignment from the Army of the Potomac as a sign of official dissatisfaction with his generalship and step up their personal attacks.

Meade grudgingly accepted the decision and dutifully soldiered on south of Petersburg. Nonetheless, this episode inflicted permanent scars on Meade's ego and, in combination with the earlier imbroglio at Spotsylvania, engendered a bitter resentment of Sheridan. When news of victories by Sheridan's forces arrived at his headquarters in September, Meade told his wife: "I am very glad for the cause and glad for Sheridan's sake; but I must confess to enough human weakness to regret this opportunity of distinction was denied me, who was, I think, from previous service and present position, entitled to it. . . . My time I suppose has passed, and I must now content myself with doing my duty unnoticed."[17]

Although peeved at his situation, at no time did Meade consider resigning in protest. In a sense he faced the same problem the administration had in determining what to do with him the previous fall and winter; namely, the lack of a better option. Out of a sense of duty and commitment to the Union, Meade was determined to contribute his military talents to the destruction of the Confederacy, and there simply was no other position available where he could do more than as commander of the Army of the Potomac. He would never be general in chief, and there were only two other Union commands to which he could be assigned that carried the importance and prestige of leading the Army of the Potomac, those in Georgia and the Shenandoah Valley. To give Meade anything less, Grant recognized, would undoubtedly be seized upon by Meade's political and military enemies as vindication of their efforts to discredit the general. And although Grant liked Meade and believed that his valuable services were underappreciated, unless Sheridan or Sherman committed a gross blunder that led to disaster, there was no way those jobs were going to be available.

Meade also stayed on because, however angry he might have been with Grant when it came to assignments, he fundamentally agreed with his conduct of the campaign. Meade had submitted his resignation on numerous occasions in 1863, largely out of frustration with the operational limitations and the (to his mind) fundamentally flawed approach the administration forced upon him. In 1864, however, Grant had made few operational decisions—and none of any consequence— that Meade disagreed with. Most importantly, the overall vision

that shaped Grant's operations in Virginia corresponded closely with Meade's. The idea of getting to the James River and
operating against Lee's communications from there was, after
all, what Meade and his fellow Army of the Potomac generals
had been championing since 1862.

Consequently, despite a bruised ego, Meade remained in command of the Army of the Potomac and the effort to get at Lee's
road and rail supply lines, which resumed in October. Grant conceived a plan whereby Butler's command would conduct a diver-
sionary attack north of the James, while Meade's Second, Fifth,
and Ninth Corps attacked the Confederate right. Parke's Ninth
Corps would move forward from the position Warren's Fifth had
established in September near the Peebles Farm and serve as a
pivot point for the other two corps. Forming on Parke's left,
Warren's corps would advance west and then swing north to hit
the Confederates facing Parke's corps. While doing so, Warren's
men would also keep an eye on their left, where the Second
Corps was to drive west until it reached Boydton Plank Road.
From there, it was hoped the offensive's momentum would carry
Union forces on to the Southside Railroad.

On October 27 Meade ordered the operation to begin.
Unfortunately, bad roads hampered the movements of Hancock's
and Warren's corps, and strong Confederate entrenchments
offered Parke little prospect of achieving a breakthrough. Despite
these problems, Hancock managed to reach Boydton Plank Road
near Burgess' Mill. There, however, he encountered the enemy in
a position that, with Warren's command bogged down by difficult
terrain, was too strong to be taken by assault. The Rebels then
launched a vicious counterattack into a gap that developed
between Warren and Hancock. Although successfully repulsed, it
convinced Hancock that he could not stay at Burgess' Mill. Thus,
with Meade's and Grant's blessing, he decided to fall back, having
gained no new ground for the Federals. "A *well*-conducted fizzle,"
was how one of Meade's staff officers described the "Sixth
Petersburg Offensive."[18]

Less than two weeks later, the 1864 presidential election
was held. As a military professional, Meade made a point of
standing aloof from the unseemly world of politics and politi-

cians. Thus, as the campaign reached a fever pitch, he viewed it as simply a distraction and did nothing "except earnestly to wish the election was over, [for] as we see, until it is, nothing else will be though[t] of and no proper thought given to the war."[19] Meade, however, could not help but recognize that he was in a position at once prominent yet awkward regarding the two presidential candidates. Certainly, he had no love for an administration and party that had done nothing but carp and slander his military reputation.

As if there was any need for a reminder of how low his stock was with Republicans, on October 13 a Radical Republican newspaper published a scathing attack against Meade. While praising Butler's less effective operations north of the James, it remarked that "South of it 'somebody blundered'—Gen. Meade, to wit; and the Army of the Potomac . . . , instead of carrying the Southside railroad, as was expected, gave up its great opportunity to the clumsiness of its leader . . . , whose incompetence, indecision, half-heartedness in the war have again and again been demonstrated." The paper did not confine its criticism of Meade only to his performance in the most recent offensive. "Let us tell the truth of him," it stated:

> He is the general who at Gettysburg bore off the laurels which belonged to Howard and to Hancock; who at Williamsport suffered a beaten army to escape him; who, when holding the line of the Rapidan, fled before Lee without a battle to the gates of the capital; who at Mine Run drew back in dismay from a conflict . . . ; who, in the campaign from the Rapidan to the James under Grant, annulled the genius of his chief by his own executive incapacity; who lost the prize of Petersburg by martinet delay . . . ; who insulted his corps commanders and his army by attributing to them that inability to co-operate with each other which was traceable solely to the unmilitary slovenliness of their general.[20]

Although some speculated this might happen, Meade had no intention of letting his mistreatment at the hands of the administration and its political friends lead him to abandon his professional ethic of nonpartisan service and support McClellan. To be sure, Meade respected McClellan as a general and did not doubt his fidelity to the Union cause. But he thought his former commander "very unfortunate in his friends and backers."[21] On election day Meade maintained a detached stance as he watched his army cast their ballots and, like Grant, did not vote himself. As he expected, the army and the North gave resounding majorities to Lincoln.

With the election now out of the way, Meade hoped that vigorous operations might be undertaken, despite the lateness of the season, for he sensed "significant signs that that our enemies are beginning to feel the exhaustion and effects of a three years' war." Meade was also no doubt motivated by a desire to accomplish something of significance that would silence his critics, particularly after the string of spectacular victories Sheridan had achieved in the Shenandoah Valley in September and October. Although willing to concede that victories of importance had been won in the Valley, Meade's wounded ego compelled him to downplay Sheridan's accomplishments in letters to his wife. "Early," he told her, "was preparing to leave the Valley, and a considerable part of his force had already gone, so that Sheridan when he attacked had greatly superior numbers. This is the secret of a great many brilliant victories."[22]

Meade's bitterness was further exacerbated when, after the election, the War Department selected Sheridan to fill the major-general vacancy in the regular army created when McClellan resigned his commission. Although pleased to see Sheridan rewarded for his services, Grant shared the distress of Meade's staff over their chief (one officer described Sheridan's promotion as "merely a piece of spite concocted in Washington")[23] and decided to go to the capital to personally lobby for Meade's promotion to major general in the regular army, which Grant had been pushing for since May.

When a friend criticized the general in chief, Meade admitted, "Grant is not without faults and weaknesses," among them an insensitivity to how his actions might reflect on or be received by others, which blinded him to the public perception caused by the fact that "[h]is coming here has resulted virtually in setting me aside, almost as effectually as if I had been removed." Nonetheless, Meade concluded: "There are many things in Grant that call for my warmest admiration, and but few that I feel called on to condemn. . . . He is a good soldier, of great force of character, honest and upright, of pure purposes, I think, without political aspirations. . . . His prominent quality is unflinching tenacity of purpose. . . . Take him all in all, he is, in my judgment, the best man the war has yet produced."[24]

Unfortunately for Meade, the lateness of the season and the slowness with which Washington was replacing the tens of thousands of veteran troops lost since May—not to mention the poor quality of those replacements that did arrive—killed any hopes for another major operation before the end of the year. In December Warren did lead the Fifth Corps on a six-day raid down the Weldon Railroad. There was also constant firing along the lines that, one officer later complained, "did not result in any appreciable modification of the lines, [although] the loss they entailed in killed and wounded was by no means trifling."[25] For the most part, however, both armies were content to spend the winter recuperating as best they could from the brutal months of combat that had commenced along the Rapidan.

The winter of 1864–65, like the previous year, would be a rough one for Meade. In addition to Congress dragging its feet on his promotion to major general in the regular army, while Meade had been battling the Rebels south of the James, his son, Sergeant, had fallen ill with tuberculosis. With operations ended for the year, the general managed to secure leave and get home to Philadelphia in December 1864. He found his son desperately ill and his wife heartbroken over the doctors' inability to do anything for him. After spending several days at his son's bedside, Meade had to return to the army in early January 1865.

Shortly after his arrival at headquarters, Meade received a piece of long-overdue good news. Thanks to a vigorous lobbying effort by Grant, on February 2 the Senate finally confirmed Meade's promotion to major general in the regular army. During the following week, he also found distraction from his son's situation in military operations; specifically, another movement to the west against Lee's supply lines. On February 4 Meade ordered Brig. Gen. David M. Gregg to take his cavalry division "to the Boydton plank road for the purpose of intercepting and capturing any of the enemy's wagon trains carrying supplies."[26] To support the cavalry, Meade directed Warren to take his corps and push west across Hatcher's Run, while the Second Corps, now under the command of General Humphreys (who was replaced as the Army of the Potomac's chief of staff by Brig. Gen. Alexander Webb) advanced to Armstrong's Mill to assist Warren.

On February 5 Meade rode out to Vaughn Road to supervise the operation. Once again, the Confederates responded to the Federal advance by launching vigorous counterattacks that afternoon. Humphreys managed to fight off the Rebels, but their attack induced Meade and Grant to call back Gregg's cavalry, which had reached Boydton Plank Road and managed to capture some Confederate wagons. The following afternoon Meade let Warren advance west along Dabney's Mill and Vaughn Roads, hoping to entice the enemy to fight outside their entrenchments. When the Rebels attacked along Dabney's Mill Road, however, they managed to drive Warren back to a fortified position along Hatcher's Run.

On February 7 Warren once again pushed his men forward despite a violent hailstorm and, Meade informed Grant, "recovered most of the ground he occupied yesterday." "As this accomplishes all I expected him to do," Meade continued, and strong Rebel works precluded a continuation of the offensive, the general directed Warren to once again fall back to Hatcher's Run. The operation, Meade reported to his wife afterward, "on the whole has been favorable to our side, and we have extended our lines some three miles to the left."[27]

If Meade believed that his confirmation as major general was evidence that he had friends in the North, the aftermath of the fighting around Dabney's Mill brought him back to reality. A week after this action, he learned that a Republican newspaper had declared the operation a failure and, "with its usual malice," wrote Meade, "puts the blame on me. . . . It is rather hard under these circumstances to be abused; but I suppose I must make up my mind to be abused by this set, never mind what happens."[28]

The general's mind, however, never wandered far from his son's situation at home. On February 21 he responded to a letter from his wife reporting that Sergeant's condition had taken a turn for the worse: "For your sake I should like to be home and for my own, but . . . My duty to you and my children requires I should retain the high command I have now."[29] That day Sergeant died. Upon learning the news, Grant sent Meade home to be with his family. He had been in Philadelphia for only three days when orders arrived from the secretary of war telling him to return to Petersburg. By February 28 Meade was back at City Point.

8

FINISHING OFF THE REBELLION

After his return to the field, Meade went to work with Grant, planning the spring offensive they hoped to commence in late March 1865, the earliest the Army of the Potomac had begun major operations since George McClellan was in command. On March 24 Grant directed General Ord to bring the bulk of the Army of the James south of the Appomattox. While Parke's corps held the lines in front of Petersburg, Ord's forces and the rest of the Army of the Potomac would mass on the Union left. Meade would then pull Humphreys's and Warren's corps from their forward trenches at Hatcher's Run and have Ord and Wright replace them. Once this had been done, Humphreys and Warren were to push southwest toward Dinwiddie Court House, while Sheridan's cavalry would cut loose completely from the rest of the Army of the Potomac, tear up the Southside and Danville Railroads, and then move south to aid Sherman in North Carolina.

On March 25, however, it was Lee who initiated the spring campaign with an attack on Parke's lines at Fort Stedman.

Although the Confederate strike achieved initial success against the Ninth Corps, the Union high command responded quickly and ordered reinforcements to the scene that restored the Federal line. "Very good results," Meade reported to his wife the next day, "we punishing the enemy severely, taking nearly three thousand prisoners and ten battle flags."[1]

Grant and Meade both recognized the victory at Fort Stedman had effectively set the stage for implementation of their plan to seize Lee's last supply lines. After waiting a few days for the roads to dry, on March 29 Meade rode to his far left to supervise Warren's and Humphreys's advances along the Quaker and Dabney's Mills Roads. Humphreys encountered light resistance, but Warren's advance provoked a Confederate counterattack that was easily repulsed. At the end of the day, both were in position to finally seize the Boydton Plank Road.

Meade immediately reported the good news to the general in chief, who then turned to Sheridan. "I now feel like ending the matter," Grant advised his young subordinate. But he decided not to let Sheridan "cut loose and go after the enemy's roads."[2] Instead, Sheridan would take his cavalry to Dinwiddie Court House. This would place the Union cavalry beyond the Confederate right flank and in a position from which it could then push north to the Southside Railroad via Five Forks. To his right, Warren and Humphreys would support the cavalry by advancing from their positions near Boydton Plank Road to White Oak Road, which connected Five Forks and Boydton Plank Road.

On March 30, despite heavy rains, Humphreys managed to reach Boydton Plank Road, while to his left Warren crossed it and managed to push his lead elements all the way to White Oak Road. (The rain and seemingly bottomless mud inspired one soldier to shout out to Warren, "Say, General, why don't you bring up the pontoons and the gun-boats?")[3] That same day Sheridan arrived at Dinwiddie Court House. Lee responded to these Union movements by dispatching cavalry and a division under Maj. Gen. George Pickett to Five Forks. On March 31 Pickett arrived at Five Forks and not only blunted Sheridan's attempt to take the position but also forced him to fall back nearly to Dinwiddie Court House.

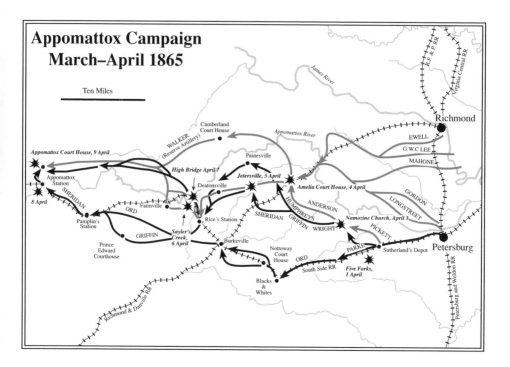

Appomattox Campaign
March–April 1865

Ten Miles

Warren's corps was nearby but had itself been in a tough fight that day along White Oak Road. Nonetheless, upon learning of Sheridan's situation, Meade recognized that an opportunity existed to catch the Rebels out in the open and deliver a decisive blow that would give the Union possession of the Southside Railroad and render the Confederate position at Petersburg untenable. "Would it not be well," he wrote Grant, "for Warren to go down with his whole corps and smash up the force in front of Sheridan? Humphreys can hold the line to the Boydton plank-road." Grant immediately agreed. "Time is of the utmost importance," Meade then advised Warren. "Use every exertion to get the troops to [Sheridan] as soon as possible."[4]

On April 1 Warren reached Five Forks and helped Sheridan launch a devastating attack that crushed the Confederate position at the crossroads. Yet due to unavoidable delays, Warren did not reach Sheridan as early as the cavalry commander expected, which led him to relieve Warren from command of the Fifth Corps and appoint Brig. Gen. Charles Griffin as his successor. After urging Sheridan and Grant to reconsider the decision and being rebuffed, Warren went to Meade. Seventeen years later a court of inquiry would conduct a thorough investigation of the matter and issue a report exonerating Warren. In April 1865, however, Meade offered no comfort to the general and told him that he and Grant had long felt Warren "was too much inclined to cavil at orders."[5] Meade added that, although he himself occasionally disagreed with Grant's instructions, he had always obeyed them.

With Lee's right shattered, Meade went to Grant and urged him to approve a plan by Sixth Corps commander Horatio Wright for an assault on the overextended Confederate right. After winning Grant's cautious approval, Meade urged Wright to go in "with all the force at your command."[6] On the morning of April 2, Wright's divisions surged forward and quickly achieved a breakthrough. With his position at Petersburg now untenable, Lee had no choice but to evacuate Richmond and Petersburg and try to escape west.

Grant was determined not to let that happen. Together he and Meade rode into Petersburg on the morning of April 3 and discussed the shape of the pursuit both hoped would result in the surrender of Lee's army. As they discussed the situation, a man was brought in who claimed to have been an engineer in the Army of Northern Virginia. He stated that Lee intended only to cross to the north bank of the Appomattox River and make his stand there. Meade, whose judgment was undoubtedly clouded by an increasingly severe head cold, was impressed by the report and suggested that they cross the Appomattox "and move against Lee in his new position." Grant disagreed and correctly divined that Lee would try to escape west, with his objective being the Richmond and Danville Railroad, which the Confederate commander could follow south to North Carolina, and then combine with Confederate forces in that state. Meade responded that, by crossing the Appomattox, the Union army could follow Lee's retreat. To this Grant replied, "we [do] not want to follow him; we [want] to get ahead of him and cut him off."[7]

HORATIO G. WRIGHT

Born Connecticut 1820; graduated U.S. Military Academy 1841, second in a class of fifty-two, commissioned 2d Lieutenant of engineers; appointed assistant to Colonel Joseph G. Totten, chief of engineers in 1856; at the outbreak of the Civil War he attempted to destroy Norfolk

Navy Yard during the Union evacuation but was captured in the attempt; after his release served as chief engineer for Samuel Heintzelman's division at First Manassas; acted as chief engineer for the Port Royal expedition in November 1861, commissioned brigadier general of volunteers on September 16, 1861; commanded a division in the disastrous assault on Secessionville (which he opposed); named commander of the Department of the Ohio in August 1862; in May 1863 given command of a division in General John Sedgwick's VI Corps of the Army of the Potomac, saw little action at Gettysburg; fought at Rappahannock Station and participated in Mine Run campaign in late 1863; led his division in the Wilderness and after Sedgwick's death at Spotsylvania on May 9, 1864, assumed command of VI Corps; on May 12, 1864, assaulted the west face of the Confederate "Mule Shoe" Salient, which became immortalized as the infamous "Bloody Angle;" appointed major general, his corps was rushed to the defense of Washington during Jubal Early's raid in July 1864, and spent the remaining summer fighting in General Phil Sheridan's conquest of the Shenandoah Valley; wounded at Cedar Creek, commanded the army until Sheridan arrived to save the day; went with the VI Corps to Petersburg; fought at Saylor's Creek and was present at Appomattox; spent the postwar years working on a variety of engineering projects, including the Brooklyn Bridge and the final construction on the Washington Monument; died in 1899, buried at Arlington National Cemetery.

Consequently, Grant decided Sheridan would take his cavalry and the Fifth Corps to Jetersville on the Richmond and Danville to deny the railroad to Lee as an escape route. A force under Ord would move to the south of Sheridan, with its objective being Burkeville on the Richmond and Danville, in case Lee eluded Sheridan. Meanwhile, Humphrey's Second and Wright's Sixth Corps, under Meade's direct command, would follow directly behind Sheridan. Although somewhat perturbed at the fact that his operations were mainly envisioned as supporting Sheridan, Meade agreed with Grant's plan.

Despite suffering from what one staff officer described as "a distressing cough and a high fever," Meade pushed his corps hard on the heels of Sheridan. On April 4 the cavalry reached Jetersville just ahead of Lee, who, due to a lack of supplies, had been compelled to stop his army at Amelia Court House longer than planned. After scouts sent toward Amelia encountered elements of Lee's command, Sheridan sent couriers back to Meade to urge his infantry forward. Meade responded with alacrity and immediately ordered Humphreys's and Wright's exhausted infantrymen to move forward "regardless of every consideration but the one of finishing the war."[8]

Unfortunately, as they tried to move to Sheridan's support on the fifth, Meade's lead corps under Humphreys found Sheridan's and Griffin's supply trains clogging the roads. Echoing his boss's growing resentment of Sheridan, one of Meade's staff officers complained: "That's the way with those cavalry bucks; they bother and howl about infantry not being up to support them, and they are precisely the people who are always blocking up the way. They are arrant boasters . . . thinking they *can* do everything and that no one else *does* do anything."[9] Thus Humphreys did not reach Jetersville until after 3:00 P.M., and Wright did not arrive until after six o'clock. Nonetheless, the infantry's arrival made the Federal line so strong that Lee was compelled to abandon his plan of moving south toward North Carolina along the railroad.

Meade, upon his arrival at Jetersville with the vanguard of Humphreys's corps, rode forward to consult with Sheridan and assume overall command of the Union forces there. He then decided to await Wright's arrival that evening and attack Lee's position at Amelia Court House with his entire force the following morning. Sheridan was exceedingly displeased at Meade's arrival and assumption of overall command (although because of his illness, Meade delegated the deployment of his corps to Sheridan). He therefore sent a note to Grant urging him to come over for a conference. Grant agreed and rode to Jetersville.

After talking with Sheridan, who predicted that if they advanced on Amelia Court House in the morning they would find Lee gone, Grant changed his plan for the morning of April 6. Agreeing that Lee would probably retreat west that night, he instructed Sheridan to take his cavalry west rather than participate in a movement against Amelia Court House. In case Lee did not retreat, however, Grant also approved Meade's plan to advance on the Confederate position along a four-mile front, with Humphreys on the left, Griffin in the center along the railroad, and Wright on the right.

The next morning, after what Sheridan later characterized as a "useless advance," Meade's men discovered that Lee had in fact already abandoned Amelia Court House and was moving west in the direction of Farmville. Quickly picking up the trail, Meade redirected Humphreys's and Griffin's marches "from a northerly to a northwesterly direction." In order to facilitate the pursuit, he also directed the Sixth Corps to face about "and moving by the left flank, [to take] position on the left of the Second."[10] With Griffin on the right, Humphreys in the center, and Wright now on the left, and Sheridan's cavalry operating to the left of Wright, Meade was able to pursue Lee much quicker.

Meade's smart redeployment of the Sixth Corps immediately paid dividends. Late in the afternoon Wright was able to catch up with the Confederate rear guard under Lt. Gen. Richard Ewell at Sayler's Creek and, aided by Humphreys's infantry and Sheridan's cavalry, destroy nearly half of Lee's command. So decisive was the victory that, as he looked on from a distance, Lee exclaimed: "My God! Has the army been dissolved?"[11]

That night Meade established his camp west of Deatonsville, but his delight in the victory at Sayler's Creek and justifiable pride in the role his skillful disposition of Wright's corps had played in bringing it about was tempered by his continuing poor health. Then to make matters worse, he got his hands on a dispatch from Sheridan claiming personal credit for the victory at Sayler's Creek. "Oh," he sarcastically exclaimed, "so *General Wright wasn't there.*" The staff officer carrying the dispatch replied, "Oh, yes, General Wright *was* there," missing entirely the tone of Meade's remark. To this, one of the general's subordinates reported, a visibly angry "Meade turned on his heel without a word."[12]

After Sayler's Creek, Sheridan's cavalry continued to race west, with Grant assigning to him the Fifth Corps and Ord's forces as well. On April 7 Meade pushed Humphreys's and Wright's corps across the Appomattox River at Farmville and High Bridge to continue his pursuit of Lee. Sheridan, meanwhile, attempted to block the Confederates' path south of the river. Sensing the end was near, Grant sent Lee a message, "asking of you the surrender of that part of that portion of the C.S. Army known as the Army of Northern Virginia." Meade wrote his wife a letter that night informing her: "It is impossible to give you a detailed account of all our operations; suffice it to say, they have been brilliantly successful, beyond the most reasonable expectations. . . . Yesterday we took over ten thousand prisoners and five generals. . . . I hear these officers virtually admit the contest is over."[13]

With Humphreys in the lead, Meade spent April 8 pursuing the remnants of the Army of Northern Virginia down the Richmond–Lynchburg Stage Road, which went through Appomattox Court House. That same day Sheridan's cavalry occupied Appomattox Station on the Southside Railroad and captured four railroad cars loaded with supplies for Lee's army. Late in the afternoon Grant caught up with Meade, and the two men decided to have dinner together at a house on the stage road known as Clifton.

Both men were in terrible physical condition. Meade was still battling the severe cold that had often compelled him to command his forces from an ambulance and no doubt contributed significantly to the poor judgment he had exhibited regarding Lee's movements since the fall of Petersburg. For his part, Grant was afflicted with a severe headache. While the two commiserated and sought relief from their respective ailments, Meade instructed Humphreys that his and Wright's corps would "move at 5 A.M. to-morrow, and the Second Corps will attack the enemy (now in its front) at once."[14] Grant, meanwhile, continued to conduct negotiations with Lee over surrender terms. With nothing having been resolved and his health still bad, Grant departed the next morning.

Afterward, Meade rode forward. He was with the Sixth Corps when he learned that Sheridan, along with Ord and Griffin, had finally blocked Lee's escape route. An aide then came up and gave Meade a note from Lee, in which the Confederate commander asked for a suspension of hostilities and an interview to discuss possible surrender terms. Meade immediately forwarded the message to Grant along with a message urging him to accept Lee's invitation to discuss terms.

After doing this, Meade continued pushing his men forward. Just east of Appomattox Court House, he managed to reach Humphreys, whose corps had made contact with the enemy. Just as Humphreys, with Meade's approval, had his men prepared to attack, Rebel horsemen rode forward to report that Lee had requested a suspension of operations pending the outcome of negotiations. Not having heard anything from Grant, Meade was skeptical and suspected the Southerners were trying to trick him. Consequently, he directed Humphreys: "Advance your skirmishers . . . and bring up your troops. We will pitch in them at once!"[15] Just then a messenger arrived from Sheridan to report that Grant had agreed to a truce. Shortly thereafter, at the McLean House in Appomattox Court House, Lee surrendered his army to Grant.

Upon hearing the news, an ecstatic Meade jubilantly rode among Wright's and Humphreys's commands. "Such a scene," one of his staff officers wrote, "I can never see again. The soldiers rushed, perfectly crazy, to the roadside, and there crowding in dense masses, shouted, screamed, yelled, threw up their hats and hopped madly up and down! . . . The noise of the cheering was such that my very ears rang. And there was General Meade galloping about and waving his cap with the best of them!"[16]

In his letters to his wife the following week, however, Meade could not help but express resentment at the way journalists showered praise and credit on Sheridan while ignoring his own contributions and those of the Army of the Potomac. "I have seen but few newspapers since this movement commenced, and don't want to see any more," he wrote his wife. "They are full of falsehood and of undue and exaggerated praise of certain individuals." Sheridan's "determination to absorb the credit of everything done," he reported, had infuriated the army, and "his conduct towards me has been beneath contempt." Meade was hopeful that this might "react against him in the minds of all just and fair-minded persons." But he was not optimistic. "I have," he told his wife, "the consciousness that I have fully performed my duty, and have done my full share of the brilliant work just completed; but if the press is determined to ignore this, and the people are determined, after four years' experience of press lying, to believe what the newspapers say, I don't see there is anything for us but to submit and be resigned."[17]

Whatever his personal faults, Sheridan had done an exemplary job during the operations around Five Forks and the pursuit to Appomattox. He had consistently anticipated the enemy's moves, reacted appropriately, and provided driving leadership to the forces under his immediate command. Meade's record after Five Forks was mixed. At Jetersville he had clearly been wrong (and Sheridan right) in his assessment of Lee's intentions for April 6. To be sure, when Meade realized he was mistaken, he handled his army with a skill that contributed greatly to the decisiveness of the action at Sayler's Creek.

Yet Jetersville was the second episode after the fall of Petersburg in which Meade made a gross miscalculation regarding the enemy's movements, the first being his prediction that Lee would make a stand north of the Appomattox after the fall of Petersburg rather than flee west. These two major errors undoubtedly attributable in large part to Meade's

illness, for they were atypical of the consistently sound operational judgment he had exercised throughout the war, he was
not without justification in believing the things he had done
right during the Appomattox Campaign deserved more attention. But his grousing and that of his staff over the praise
Grant and Sheridan received, though understandable, was mis-
placed. Grant and Sheridan deserved the accolades.

Meade at least found much to inspire hope for the future of
the Union in the aftermath of Lee's surrender. During visits to
the Confederate camps, he talked to a number of Southern
generals and government officials, including both Lee and
Longstreet. In fact, when Meade greeted Lee, the Confederate
commander did not recognize his old colleague from the antebellum army. When Meade identified himself, Lee remarked,
"What are you doing with all that grey in your beard?" Meade
jovially replied, "You have to answer for most of it!"[18]

Like Grant, Meade came away from such visits full of optimism that a quick end to the war and an enduring sectional
reconciliation were within easy reach. The Southerners "were
all affable and cordial," Meade informed his wife, "and uni-
formly said that, if any conciliatory policy was extended to the
South, peace would be at once made." A few days later he proclaimed: "It remains for statesmen, if we have any, to bring the
people of the South back to their allegiance. I am myself for
conciliation, as the policy most likely to effect a speedy
reunion. . . . We of the army have done our work; the military
power of the Rebellion is shattered."[19]

EPILOGUE

"I have a great contempt for history," Meade proclaimed in a letter to his wife the day after Lee's surrender.[1] During the weeks following Appomattox, Meade would have the satisfaction of a series of lavish receptions in his native Philadelphia, participation in the Grand Review in Washington, and being awarded an honorary doctorate from Harvard. Yet during this time, he could not ignore the fact that the first draft of history that appeared in the newspapers focused mainly on Grant's and Sheridan's contributions to the defeat of Lee's army while slighting the Army of the Potomac high command. Nor could Meade fail to sense that this was laying the foundation for a popular interpretation of the Union war effort that was distinctly unflattering to himself and his fellow eastern generals.

According to this interpretation, which continues to dominate the historical literature on the war, President Lincoln was a great and determined war leader, with questions regarding his wisdom and military judgment rendered impolitic by his martyrdom at the moment of victory. For nearly three years of fighting, even the president's wisdom and the bravery of the men in the ranks could not overcome the timidity and incompetence of the Army of the Potomac high command. Too conservative and gentlemanly to conduct operations with the aggressiveness and ruthlessness that modern total war (and Lincoln) demanded, time and again commanders like George McClellan and George Meade, as historian James M. McPherson wrote in his 1988 Pulitzer Prize–winning book *Battle Cry of Freedom,* "threw away chances in the East." But in 1864, generals finally arrived in Virginia who shared Lincoln's military sentiments. Under the driving leadership of Ulysses Grant and Philip Sheridan, the Army of the Potomac's fighting spirit was finally unleashed after being suppressed far too long by commanders who, in the words of historian T. Harry Williams, "lacked the hardness to wage hard modern war."[2] Only when this happened was the Union finally on the road to victory.

The great question for the Union effort in the East was not, however, over whether or not to wage war in a "modern" fashion. Indeed, in their respect for the power of the tactical defensive and appreciation for the importance of organization and logistics, Meade and other Army of the Potomac generals were quite "modern" in their military outlook. Ironically, from their profound understanding of the tactical and operational imperatives of warfare flowed many of the troubles they faced in formulating and executing operational and tactical plans, for it created problems rooted in another reality of modern war: the fact that popular sentiment, filtered through partisan politics, must always be taken into account.

The modern approach that Meade and his fellow Army of the Potomac generals took to operations clashed profoundly with the expectations and demands of Republican politicians. These Meade (and not inaccurately) perceived to be rooted in partisan political interests and a profound ignorance of the realities of modern warfare. Consequently, the Army of the Potomac's leadership often found itself waging two wars. The first, of course, was with Gen. Robert E. Lee's Army of Northern Virginia; the second was with their political masters in Washington. Although matters such as emancipation and command assignments played a significant role in creating tension between politicians and Army of the Potomac gener-

ABRAHAM LINCOLN

Born Kentucky 1809; received little formal education; family moved to Illinois where he held various clerking jobs; studied law; served in state legislature as a Whig; settled in Springfield, practiced law, and in 1842 married Mary Todd; retired from public life after one term in U.S. Congress, 1847–49; joined Republican party in 1856 and entered the growing debate over sectionalism; in 1858 beaten for U.S. Senate by Stephen A. Douglas, but emerged from their famous debate a national figure; nominated by Republicans and elected president in 1860; determined to preserve Union; issued Emancipation Proclamation after Union victory at Antietam in 1862; reelected in 1864; mortally wounded by John Wilkes Booth April 14, 1865; died the next day.

als, for Meade the most important issue was the question of what line of operations the Federals should adopt in Virginia.

In 1862, his analysis of operational and tactical realities in northern Virginia, the influence of fellow West Point graduates, and his own training and experiences in the region convinced Meade that the James River was by far the Army of the Potomac's best line of operations. The army Meade served with (and would ultimately command) enjoyed its greatest advantages over its Confederate foe in artillery, engineering, and manpower, assets that made it best suited to siege warfare and fighting set-piece battles, such as the one Meade intended to fight at Pipe Creek and ended up fighting at Gettysburg in July 1863. They also made it critical that the army always have secure logistics. These factors invariably made the Army of the Potomac slower and less flexible operationally, and thus less effective in the open field, than the smaller and more mobile Army of Northern Virginia.

Using the James River, Meade recognized—as did Grant and Lee—played to the Union's strengths and negated those of the Confederacy. It provided a Federal commander with the secure logistical support he needed to provision his army and gave him the ability to, as Lee complained in 1862, "take position from position, under cover of his heavy guns, & we cannot get at him without storming his works. . . . It will require 100,000 men to resist the regular siege of Richmond, which perhaps would only prolong not save it."[3]

In contrast, it was almost impossible for Meade to fight the Rebels on favorable terms north of Richmond unless Lee made an uncharacteristically gross mistake that gave the Federals an opportunity to fight on their terms, as he did at Gettysburg and as Meade hoped he would during the Bristoe Station Campaign. By the fall of 1862, however, the inability and/or unwillingness of the Northern public and politicians to see military realities the way Meade and other West Pointers did induced the Lincoln administration to decide that the Army of the Potomac could no longer use the James. The consequences of this decision were defeats at Fredericksburg and Chancellorsville and, during Meade's tenure in command, the retreat to Centreville, the minor victories at Rappahannock Station and Kelly's Ford, and the abortive Mine Run operation. For Grant, the cost of following the Lincoln administration's operational wishes in 1864 before he could operate from the James was a butcher's bill so large that it would do inestimable damage to his reputation as a general.

Meade, of course, understood that war is always shaped by political considerations. Yet he scrupulously avoided the political world, in line with a concept of military professionalism that had been instilled in him during his years in the antebellum army. This ethic viewed the military officer as an apolitical implementer of policy, not a political shaper of it. Ideally, in exchange for deferring to political leaders in the formation of policy, their supposed area of expertise, military officers would be deferred to in their area of expertise, military planning and command. Of course, the reality of the Union military and political system, in which political and military spheres of influence either were blurred or overlapped and the fact that members of the Lincoln administration and Congress had no intention of giving West Point professionals a free hand in anything, made any hope that Washington would accept and respect such a division of responsibility completely unrealistic.

Meade was not blind to this fact. Nonetheless, although he had a low opinion of politicians and was constantly exasperated by their interference in what he considered strictly military matters, he made a point of living up to his end of the bargain. He left policy to Washington and made no effort to influence debates inside or outside the army over strictly political matters, such as the treatment of Southern property and the presidential contest of 1864. Nor did Meade participate in the campaigns within the army to remove generals the administration had seen fit to place over him in command, even though in the cases of Ambrose Burnside and Joseph Hooker such cabals were quite justifiable and he privately agreed with their ends.

In working with Henry Halleck and Lincoln in 1863, Meade clearly accepted that, while it was his job to offer suggestions, the final decision as to what policy he was to implement always rested with them. When he found himself in fundamental disagreement with the operational ideas imposed on him by the Lincoln administration, Meade did not attempt to work around his superiors by cultivating political sponsors (something Grant did with great skill) or taking his complaints to the press. Instead, he offered his resignation.

Meade continued to steer clear from the process of shaping political and public opinion after the war. Unlike many generals on both sides, he made little effort to shape public perceptions of the war and his role in it. He had no interest in writing his memoirs, and during the war he had made far too many irreconcilable enemies in both the press and the Republican party to hope for charity from either. Consequently, few outside the general's inner circle of associates stood up publicly for Meade as the first histories of the war were being written and published. As a result the general quickly became the man who benefited from whichever "fatal" Confederate mistake at Gettysburg happened to be the subject of debate among Southerners at any particular time and whose feckless performance afterward made it necessary for Lincoln to place "his man" Grant in command. Little attention would be paid to the fact that Grant's operations in 1864–65 to a large extent vindicated Meade's arguments that the way to achieve victory in Virginia was not north of Richmond, as Lincoln, Halleck, and Republican politicians in Washington believed, but south and east of the city by operating from the James River.

The years after Appomattox would be ones of frustration for Meade as he watched his significant contributions to Union victory being denigrated, minimized, or ignored altogether. Nonetheless, he continued to soldier on in the service of his country. As the nation's fourth-ranking major general, Meade's first postwar assignment was command of the Division of the Atlantic, headquartered at Philadelphia. In this office he helped resolve a crisis sparked by raids across the Canadian border by armed Americans belonging to a branch of the Irish Fenian Society.

In 1867 he went south to replace John Pope as commander of U.S. occupation forces in Georgia, Florida, and Alabama. Meade did not want the job and regretted that the rest of the nation seemed to have failed to embrace the spirit of sectional reconciliation that had prevailed at Appomattox. He had no doubt what the problem was. "I am very sorry to see," he complained, "that *political passion* is again assuming the ascendancy, and that, blinded by this malign influence, both sides are plunging into the same evil courses which originated the war . . . , blended so intimately with the questions, not only of *politics*, but of *party*."[4] Meade attempted to counter this by adopting moderate-to-conservative policies and working through his friendships with former Confederate war leaders. This, of course, did little to advance the cause of justice for the freedmen, and Meade once again found himself being criticized by the same members of the radical wing of the Republican party who had tormented him during the war.

After Grant assumed the presidency in 1869, Meade was relieved of duty in the South and once again took command of the Division of the Atlantic. This change, although it pleased him to once again be back in his hometown, was accompanied by yet another slight. When Grant became president and Sherman assumed command of the army with the rank of general, Sheridan, not Meade, was chosen as Sherman's successor as lieutenant general.

Dull routine characterized Meade's professional life after 1869. He received much personal gratification, however, from participation in activities of the Society of the Army of the Potomac and involvement in several civic-improvement projects in Philadelphia. Unfortunately, he also suffered several attacks of pneumonia during this period, a lingering effect of the wounds he had received as a brigade commander at Glendale in June 1862. A little over a decade after that battle, pneumonia sent the Army of the Potomac's final commander to his bed for the last time. On November 6, 1872, George Gordon Meade died, a victim of wounds suffered on the Virginia Peninsula, where he had so badly wanted to lead the Army of the Potomac and that had figured so prominently in the war in the East.

Notes

Introduction

1. Herman Hattaway and Archer Jones, *How the North Won: A Military History of the Civil War* (Urbana: University of Illinois Press, 1983), 405; Charles Wainwright, *A Diary of Battle: The Personal Journals of Colonel Charles S. Wainwright, 1861–1865,* ed. Allan Nevins (New York: Harcourt, 1962), 219; Meade to his wife, May 19, 1863, *The Life and Letters of George Gordon Meade, Major-General United States Army,* ed. George Gordon Meade, 2 vols. (New York: Charles Scribner's Sons, 1913), 1:377 [hereafter cited as *Letters*].

2. Charles F. Benjamin, "Hooker's Appointment and Removal," in *Battles and Leaders of the Civil War,* eds. Robert U. Johnson and Clarence C. Buel, 4 vols. (New York: Century, 1887), 2:243.

1. Cadiz to Detroit

1. William B. Skelton, *An American Profession of Arms: The Army Officer Corps, 1784–1861* (Lawrence: University Press of Kansas, 1992), 167.

2. Meade to his wife, May 27, July 9, 1846, *Letters,* 1:91, 109–10.

3. Meade to his wife, May 27, 1846, ibid., 91.

4. Meade to his wife, June 12, 1846, ibid., 102.

2. Army of the Potomac

1. Meade to his wife, Jan. 2, Feb. 11, 1862, *Letters,* 1:242, 246.

2. McClellan to Edwin Stanton, [Feb. 3,] 1862, *Civil War Papers of George B. McClellan: Selected Correspondence, 1860–1865,* ed. Stephen W. Sears (New York: Ticknor and Fields, 1989), 164, 166–67, 169.

3. Meade to his wife, Mar. 9, 1862, *Letters,* 1:250.

4. Meade to his wife, Apr. 4, 8, 1862, ibid., 256, 257.

5. Meade to his wife, June 18, 1862, ibid., 276.

6. Meade to his wife, June 22, 1862, ibid., 277–78.

7. Meade to his wife, Aug. 16, 1862, ibid., 303.

8. Meade to his wife, Sept. 3, 1862, ibid., 307–8.

9. Meade to Joseph Dickinson, Sept. 24, 1862, in U.S. War Department, *The War of the Rebellion: A Compilation of the Official Records of the Union and Confederate Armies,* 70 vols. in 128 pts. (Washington, D.C.: Government Printing Office, 1880–1901), 19(1):268 [hereafter cited as *OR;* all references are from series 1 unless otherwise noted]; Daniel H. Hill, "The Battle of South Mountain, or Boonsboro," in *Battles and Leaders,* 2:574.

10. Hooker to Seth Williams, Nov. 8, 1862, *OR,* 19(1):218.

11. Meade to his wife, Oct. 20, 1862, *Letters,* 1:320; Meade to John Sergeant Meade, Oct. 23, 1862, ibid.

12. Meade to his wife, Oct. 12, 1862, ibid., 319.

3. Division and Corps Command

1. Meade to his wife, Nov. 13, 1862, *Letters,* 1:326–27.

2. Meade to his wife, Nov. 22, 1862, ibid., 330.

3. Wainwright, *Diary of Battle,* 143; Frank A. O'Reilly, *"Stonewall" Jackson at Fredericksburg: The Battle of Prospect Hill, December 13, 1862* (Lynchburg, VA: H. E. Howard, 1993), 33.

4. George C. Rable, *Fredericksburg! Fredericksburg!* (Chapel Hill: University of North Carolina Press, 2002), 216.

5. Meade to his wife, Dec. 20, 1862, *Letters,* 1:340–41.

6. Meade to his wife, Jan. 23, 1863, ibid., 348.

7. Meade to his wife, Jan. 26, 1863, ibid., 351.

8. John Bigelow, *Chancellorsville* (1910; reprint, New York: Smithmark, 1995), 221.

9. General Orders No. 47, Apr. 30, 1863, *OR,* 25(1):171; Bigelow, *Chancellorsville,* 236–37.

10. Meade's report, May 12, 1863, *OR,* 25(1):507.

11. Freeman Cleaves, *Meade of Gettysburg* (Norman: University of Oklahoma Press, 1960), 108; Darius N. Couch, "The Chancellorsville Campaign," in *Battles and Leaders,* 3:161; Biddle to his wife, May 9, 1863, James Cornell Biddle Papers, Historical Society of Pennsylvania, Philadelphia.

12. James Biddle to his wife, May 17, 1863, Biddle Papers; Couch, "Chancellorsville Campaign," 3:171.

13. Meade to his wife, May 12, 1863, *Letters,* 1:374–75.

14. Cleaves, *Meade of Gettysburg,* 118.

15. Meade to his wife, June 25, 1863, *Letters,* 1:389.

16. Ibid., 388.

4. Gettysburg Commander

1. T. Harry Williams, *Lincoln and His Generals* (New York: Alfred A. Knopf, 1952), 258; Hattaway and Jones, *How the North Won,* 400.

2. Benjamin, "Hooker's Appointment and Removal," in *Battles and Leaders,* 3:241.

3. Halleck to Meade, June 27, 1863, *OR,* 27(1):61.

4. Benjamin, "Hooker's Appointment and Removal," 3:243; Meade to Halleck, June 28, 1863, *OR,* 27(1):61; Halleck to Meade, June 28, 1863, ibid., 62.

5. Williams, *Lincoln and his Generals,* 260; William Swinton, *Army of the Potomac* (1866; reprint, New York: Smithmark, 1995), 324; Wainwright, *Diary of Battle,* 227; Emory M. Thomas, *Robert E. Lee: A Biography* (New York: W. W. Norton, 1995), 293.

6. Meade to Halleck, June 30, 1863, *OR,* 27(1):67.

7. Circular, Headquarters, Army of the Potomac, June 30, 1863, *OR,* 27(3):415.

8. Edwin Stanton to Meade, June 30, 1863, *OR,* 27(1):69; Meade to his wife, June 30, 1863, *Letters,* 2:18.

9. Meade to Halleck, July 1, 1863, *OR,* 27(1):71.

10. Circular, Headquarters, Army of the Potomac, July 1, 1863, *OR,* 27(3):458–59.

11. Henry J. Hunt, "The First Day at Gettysburg," in *Battles and Leaders,* 3:274; Hunt, "The Second Day at Gettysburg," in ibid., 291.

12. Meade, *Letters,* 2:36.

13. Butterfield to Hancock, July 1, 1863, *OR,* 27(3):461.

14. Cleaves, *Meade of Gettysburg,* 148.

15. John Gibbon, "The Council of War on the Second Day," in *Battles and Leaders,* 3:314.

16. Frank L. Byrne and Andrew T. Weaver, eds., *Haskell of Gettysburg: His Life and Civil War Papers* (Kent, OH: The Kent State University Press, 1989 [1970]), 166.

17. Meade to Smith, July 5, 1863, *OR,* 27(3):539; General Orders No. 68, July 4, 1863, ibid., 519.

18. Lincoln to Halleck, July 7, 1863, in *Collected Works of Abraham Lincoln,* ed. Roy P. Basler, 9 vols. (New Brunswick, NJ: Rutgers University Press, 1955), 6:319 [hereafter cited as *CWAL*]; Lincoln to Halleck, July 6, 1863, *OR,* 27(3):567.

19. Halleck to Meade, July 13, 1863, *OR,* 27(1):92.

20. Henry J. Hunt, "The Third Day at Gettysburg," *Battles and Leaders,* 3:382; Wainwright, *Diary of Battle,* 261.

21. Williams, *Lincoln and His Generals,* 268; Lincoln to Meade, July 14, 1863, *CWAL,* 327–28.

22. Meade to his wife, July 14, 1863, *Letters,* 2:134.

23. Meade to his wife, July 18, 1863, ibid., 136.

5. Autumn Maneuvers

1. Lincoln to Meade, Sept. 15, 1863, *OR,* 29(2):187; Halleck to Meade, Sept. 15, 1863, ibid.

2. Meade to Halleck, Sept. 18, 1863, ibid., 201–2.

3. Halleck to Meade, Sept. 19, 1863, ibid., 206–7; Lincoln to Halleck, Sept. 19, 1863, ibid., 207–8.

4. Meade to his wife, Sept. 24, 1863, *Letters,* 2:150.

5. Halleck to Meade, Sept. 24, 1863, *OR,* 29(1):147.

6. Lee to Seddon, Oct. 11, 1863, ibid., 405.

7. Meade to his wife, Oct. 30, Nov. 3, 1863, *Letters,* 2:154–55.

8. Halleck to Meade, Oct. 18, 1863, *OR,* 29(2):346; Theodore Lyman, *Meade's Headquarters, 1863–1865: Letters of Colonel Theodore Lyman from the Wilderness to Appomattox,* ed. George R. Agassiz (Boston: *Atlantic Monthly,* 1922), 31.

9. Meade to Halleck, Oct. 18, 1863, *OR,* 29(2):346.

10. Wainwright, *Diary of Battle,* 284.

11. Francis A. Donaldson to his brother, Oct. 22, 1863, in Donaldson, *Inside the Army of the Potomac: The Civil War Experience of Captain Francis Adams Donaldson,* ed. J. Gregory Acken (Mechanicsburg, PA: Stackpole, 1998), 371.

12. Meade to his wife, Oct. 23, 1863, *Letters,* 2:154.

13. Robert McAllister to his family, Oct. 25, Nov. 11, 1863, in *The Civil War Letters of General Robert McAllister,* ed. James I . Robertson Jr. (New Brunswick, NJ: Rutgers University Press, 1965), 350, 357; George T. Stevens, *Three Years in the Sixth Corps* (Albany, NY: S. R. Gray, 1866), 290.

14. Biddle to his wife, Oct. 12, 23, 1863, Biddle Papers.

15. Meade to Halleck, Nov. 2, 1863, *OR,* 29(2):409.

16. Halleck to Meade, Nov. 3, 1863, ibid., 412.

17. Donaldson, *Inside the Army of the Potomac,* 393; Meade to his wife, Nov. 9, 1863, *Letters,* 2:155.

18. Lincoln to Meade, Nov. 9, 1863, *CWAL,* 7:7.

19. Meade to his wife, Dec. 2, 1863, *Letters,* 2:157.

20. Biddle to his wife, Dec. 1, 1863, Biddle Papers, HSP.

21. Warren to Williams, Dec. 3, 1863, *OR,* 29(1):698; Warren to Meade, Nov. 30, 1863, *OR,* 29(2):517.

22. Lyman, *Meade's Headquarters,* 56; Martin T. McMahon, "From Gettysburg to the Coming of Grant," in *Battles and Leaders,* 4:91.

23. Meade to Halleck, Dec. 2, 1863, *OR,* 29(1):12.

24. Henry Matrau to his mother, Dec. 7, 1863, in *Letters Home: Henry Matrau of the Iron Brigade,* ed. Marcia Reid-Green (Lincoln: University of Nebraska Press, 1993), 71; Donaldson, *Inside the Army of the Potomac,* 406; David M. Jordan, *"Happiness Is Not My Companion": The Life of General G.K. Warren* (Bloomington: Indiana University Press, 2001), 116.

25. Meade to his wife, Dec. 2, 1863, *Letters,* 2:158.

26. Meade to his wife, Dec. 7, 1863, ibid., 160.

6. With Grant to the James

1. William F. Smith, *Autobiography of Major General William F. Smith,* ed. Herbert M. Schiller (Dayton, OH: Morningside, 1990), 83.

2. James Biddle to his wife, Mar. 20, 1864, Biddle Papers, HSP; Ulysses S. Grant, *Personal Memoirs of U. S. Grant,* 2 vols. (New York: Charles L. Webster, 1885), 2:404–5.

3. Meade to his wife, Mar. 14, 1864, *Letters,* 2:178.

4. Grant to Halleck, Jan. 19, 1864, *OR,* 33(1):394–95.

5. Halleck to Grant, Feb. 17, 1864, *OR*, 32(2):411–13.

6. Grant, *Memoirs*, 2:416.

7. Grant to Butler, Apr. 2, 1864, *OR*, 36(1):16.

8. Meade to Bowers, Nov. 1, 1864, ibid., 189.

9. Horace Porter, *Campaigning with Grant* (New York: Century, 1897), 37; Meade to his wife, Apr. 13, 1864, *Letters*, 2:189.

10. Meade to his wife, Mar. 26, Apr. 13, 1864, *Letters*, 183, 189.

11. Meade to Grant, May 5, 1864, *OR*, 36(2):403.

12. Cleaves, *Meade of Gettysburg*, 237; Grant to Meade, May 5, 1864, *OR*, 36(2):403.

13. Meade to Bowers, Nov. 1, 1864, *OR*, 36(1):189.

14. Lyman, *Meade's Headquarters*, 94.

15. Grant to Halleck, May 8, 1864, *OR*, 36(1):3; Grant to Meade, May 7, 1864, *OR*, 36(2):481; Grant, *Memoirs*, 2:463.

16. Philip H. Sheridan, *Personal Memoirs of P. H. Sheridan*, 2 vols. (New York: D. Appleton, 1888), 1:368–69.

17. Porter, *Campaigning with Grant*, 84.

18. Andrew A. Humphreys, *The Virginia Campaign of 1864 and 1865* (New York: Charles Scribner's Sons, 1883), 110.

19. Meade to his wife, May 19, 1864, *Letters*, 2:197.

20. Abner R. Small, *The Road to Richmond: The Civil War Memoirs of Maj. Abner R. Small of the 16th Maine Vols.*, ed. Harold Adams Small (Berkeley: University of California Press, 1957), 146–47.

21. Porter, *Campaigning with Grant*, 114–15; Grant to Edwin Stanton, May 13, 1864, in Grant, *Memoirs*, 2:478.

22. Meade to his wife, May 19, 1864, *Letters*, 2:197–98.

23. Meade to his wife, May 23, 1864, ibid., 198; William T. Sherman to Edwin Stanton, May 23, 1864, *OR*, 38(4):294; Lyman, *Meade's Headquarters*, 126.

24. Bruce Catton, *Grant Takes Command* (Boston: Little, Brown, 1968), 247.

25. Meade to his wife, May 29, 1864, *Letters*, 2:199; Grant to Meade, June 3, 1864, *OR*, 36(3):526.

26. Meade to his wife, June 5, 1864, *Letters*, 2:201.

7. Petersburg

1. Meade to his wife, May 23, June 1, 1864, *Letters,* 2:198.

2. Meade to his wife, June 12, 1864, ibid., 204; Thomas, *Robert E. Lee,* 339.

3. Charles Dana to Edwin Stanton, June 15, 1864, *OR,* 40(1):19–20; Robert McAllister to his wife, June 15, 1864, in *Civil War Letters,* 441.

4. Meade to Bowers, Nov. 1, 1864, *OR,* 40(2):168.

5. Porter, *Campaigning with Grant,* 209.

6. Wainwright, *Diary of Battle,* 424–25; Lyman, *Meade's Headquarters,* 170.

7. Meade to Grant, June 20, 1864, *OR,* 40(2):233.

8. Burnside's testimony, Court of Inquiry on the Mine Explosion, Aug. 10, 1864, *OR,* 40(1):60; William H. Powell, "The Battle of the Petersburg Crater," *Battles and Leaders,* 4:548.

9. Orders, Headquarters Army of the Potomac, July 29, 1864, *OR,* 40(1):135; Humphreys, *Virginia Campaign,* 252, 254.

10. Meade to Burnside, July 30, 1864, *OR,* 40(1):141.

11. Porter, *Campaigning with Grant,* 267.

12. Meade to his wife, Aug. 10, 1864, *Letters,* 2:221.

13. Finding, Court of Inquiry on the Mine Explosion, Sept. 9, 1864, *OR,* 40(1):127.

14. Meade to Theodore S. Bowers, Nov. 1, 1864, *OR,* 42(1):30.

15. Meade to his wife, July 29, 1864, *Letters,* 2:216–17.

16. Meade to his wife, Aug. 13, 1864, ibid., 221.

17. Meade to his wife, Sept. 22, 1864, ibid., 229.

18. Lyman, *Meade's Headquarters,* 251.

19. Meade to his wife, Oct. 7, 1864, *Letters,* 2:232.

20. "The War in Virginia," *New York Independent,* Oct. 13, 1864, quoted in ibid., 342.

21. Meade to his wife, Oct. 7, 1864, ibid., 232.

22. Meade to his wife, Nov. 17, 1864, ibid., 243; Meade to his wife, Sept. 27, 1864, ibid., 230.

23. James Biddle to his wife, Nov. 18, 1864, Biddle Papers, HSP.

24. Meade to his wife, Nov. 24, 1864, *Letters,* 2:246.

25. Humphreys, *Virginia Campaign,* 316.

26. Circular, Headquarters, Army of the Potomac, Feb. 4, 1865, *OR,* 42(2):370–71.

27. Meade to Grant, Feb. 7, 1865, ibid., 448; Meade to his wife, Feb. 7, 1865, *Letters,* 2:261.

28. Meade to his wife, Feb. 11, 1865, *Letters,* 2:262.

29. Meade to his wife, Feb. 21, 1865, ibid., 264.

8. Finishing Off the Rebellion

1. Meade to his wife, Mar. 26, 1865, *Letters,* 2:268.

2. Grant to Sheridan, Mar. 29, 1865, *OR,* 46(3):266.

3. Warren Lee Goss, *Recollections of a Private: A Story of the Army of the Potomac* (New York: Thomas Y. Cromwell, 1890), 341.

4. Meade to Grant, Mar. 31, 1865, *OR,* 46(3):341; Meade to Warren, Mar. 31, 1865, ibid., 367.

5. Jordan, *"Happiness Is Not My Companion,"* 234.

6. Meade to Wright, Apr. 1, 1865, *OR,* 46(3):422.

7. Grant, *Memoirs,* 2:610.

8. Lyman, *Meade's Headquarters,* 345; Meade to the army, Apr. 4, 1865, *OR,* 46(3):549.

9. Lyman, *Meade's Headquarters,* 346.

10. Sheridan, *Personal Memoirs,* 2:179; Meade to Grant, Apr. 6, 1865, *OR,* 46(3):597.

11. Thomas, *Robert E. Lee,* 358.

12. Lyman, *Meade's Headquarters,* 351.

13. Grant to Lee, Apr. 7, 1865, *OR,* 46(1):56; Meade to his wife, Apr. 7, 1865, *Letters,* 2:270.

14. Webb to Humphreys, Apr. 8, 1865, *OR,* 46(3):645.

15. Lyman, *Meade's Headquarters,* 357.

16. Ibid., 358.

17. Meade to his wife, Apr. 10, 12, 1865, *Letters,* 2:271.

18. Lyman, *Meade's Headquarters,* 360.

19. Meade to his wife, Apr. 10, 22, 1865, *Letters,* 2:270, 275.

Epilogue

1. Meade to his wife, Apr. 10, 1865, *Letters,* 2:271.

2. James M. McPherson, *Battle Cry of Freedom: The Civil War Era* (New York: Oxford University Press, 1988), 857; Williams, *Lincoln and His Generals,* 261.

3. Lee to Davis, June 5, 1862, in *The Wartime Papers of Robert E. Lee,* ed. Clifford Dowdey and Louis H. Manarin (Boston: Little, Brown, 1961), 184

4. Meade, *Letters,* 2:290.

Selected Bibliography

Ambrose, Stephen E. *Halleck: Lincoln's Chief of Staff.* Baton Rouge: Louisiana State University Press, 1962.

Biddle, James Cornell. Papers. Historical Society of Pennsylvania, Philadelphia.

Bigelow, John. *Chancellorsville.* 1910. Reprint, New York: Smithmark, 1995.

Boritt, Gabor S., ed. *Lincoln's Generals.* New York: Oxford University Press, 1995.

Catton, Bruce. *Mr. Lincoln's Army.* Garden City, NY: Doubleday, 1951.

_____. *Glory Road.* Garden City, NY: Doubleday, 1952.

_____. *A Stillness at Appomattox.* Garden City, NY: Doubleday, 1953.

_____. *Grant Takes Command.* Boston: Little, Brown, 1968.

Cleaves, Freeman. *Meade of Gettysburg.* Norman: University of Oklahoma Press, 1960.

Coddington, Edward. "The Strange Reputation of George G. Meade: A Lesson in Historiography." *The Historian* 23 (1962): 145–66.

_____. *The Gettysburg Campaign: A Study in Command.* New York: Charles Scribner's Sons, 1968.

Donald, David Herbert. *Lincoln.* New York: Simon and Schuster, 1995.

Donaldson, Francis A. *Inside the Army of the Potomac: The Civil War Experience of Captain Francis Adams Donaldson,* edited by J. Gregory Acken. Mechanicsburg, PA: Stackpole, 1998.

Gallagher, Gary W., ed. *Lee the Soldier.* Lincoln: University of Nebraska Press, 1996.

Goss, Warren Lee. *Recollections of a Private: A Story of the Army of the Potomac.* New York: Thomas Y. Cromwell, 1890.

Graham, Martin F., and George F. Skoch. *Mine Run: A Campaign of Lost Opportunities.* Lynchburg, VA: H.E. Howard, 1987.

Grant, Ulysses S. *Personal Memoirs of Ulysses S. Grant.* 2 vols. New York: Charles L. Webster, 1885.

Hagerman, Edward. *The American Civil War and the Origins of Modern Warfare: Ideas, Organization, and Field Command.* Bloomington: Indiana University Press, 1988.

Hattaway, Herman. *Shades of Blue and Gray: An Introductory Military History of the Civil War.* Columbia: University of Missouri Press, 1997.

Hattaway, Herman, and Archer Jones. *How the North Won: A Military History of the Civil War.* Urbana: University of Illinois Press, 1983.

Hebert, Walter H. *Fighting Joe Hooker.* New York: Bobbs-Merril, 1944.

Henderson, William D. *Road to Bristoe Station: Campaigning with Lee and Meade, August 1–October 20, 1863.* Lynchburg, VA: H. E. Howard, 1987.

Hennessy, John J. "'We Shall Make Richmond Howl': The Army of the Potomac on the Eve of Chancellorsville." In *Chancellorsville: The Battle and its Aftermath,* edited by Gary W. Gallagher, 1–35. Chapel Hill: University of North Carolina Press, 1996.

_____. "'I Dread the Spring': The Army of the Potomac Prepares for the Overland Campaign." In *The Wilderness Campaign,* edited by Gary W. Gallagher, 66–105. Chapel Hill: University of North Carolina Press, 1997.

Humphreys, Andrew A. *From Gettysburg to the Rapidan.* New York: Charles Scribner's Sons, 1883.

_____. *The Virginia Campaign of 1864 and 1865.* New York: Charles Scribner's Sons, 1883.

Johnson, Robert U., and Clarence C. Buel, eds. *Battles and Leaders of the Civil War.* 4 vols. New York: Century, 1887.

Jones, Archer. *Civil War Command and Strategy: The Process of Victory and Defeat.* New York: Free Press, 1992.

Jordan, David M. *"Happiness Is Not My Companion": The Life of General G.K. Warren.* Bloomington: Indiana University Press, 2001.

Lincoln, Abraham. *The Collected Works of Abraham Lincoln,* edited by Roy P. Basler. 9 vols. New Brunswick, NJ: Rutgers University Press, 1953–55.

Lyman, Theodore. *Meade's Headquarters, 1863–1865: Letters of Colonel Theodore Lyman from Wilderness to Appomattox,* edited by George R. Agassiz. Boston: *Atlantic Monthly,* 1922.

Matrau, Henry. *Letters Home: Henry Matrau of the Iron Brigade,* edited by Marcia Reid-Green. Lincoln: University of Nebraska Press, 1993.

McAllister, Robert. *The Civil War Letters of General Robert McAllister,* edited by James I. Robertson. New Brunswick, NJ: Rutgers University Press, 1965.

McClellan, George B. *McClellan's Own Story: The War for the Union, the Soldiers Who Fought It, the Civilians Who Directed It, and His Relations to It and to Them.* Edited by William C. Prime. New York: Charles L. Webster, 1887.

_____. *Civil War Papers of George B. McClellan: Selected Correspondence, 1860–1865,* edited by Stephen W. Sears. New York: Ticknor and Fields, 1989.

McPherson, James M. *Battle Cry of Freedom: The Civil War Era.* New York: Oxford University Press, 1988.

Meade, George Gordon, ed. *The Life and Letters of George Gordon Meade, Major-General United States Army.* 2 vols. New York: Charles Scribner's Sons, 1913.

O'Reilly, Frank. *"Stonewall" Jackson at Fredericksburg: The Battle of Prospect Hill, December 13, 1862.* Lynchburg, VA: H.E. Howard, 1993.

Paludan, Phillip S. *"A People's Contest": The Union and the Civil War, 1861–1865.* New York: Harper and Row, 1988.

Porter, Horace. *Campaigning with Grant.* New York: Century, 1897.

Rable, George S. *Fredericksburg! Fredericksburg!* Chapel Hill: University of North Carolina Press, 2002.

Rhea, Gordon C. *The Battle of the Wilderness, May 5–6, 1864.* Baton Rouge: Louisiana State University Press, 1994.

_____. *The Battles for Spotsylvania Court House and the Road to Yellow Tavern, May 7–12, 1864.* Baton Rouge: Louisiana State University Press, 1997.

_____. *To the North Anna River: Grant and Lee, May 13–25, 1864.* Baton Rouge: Louisiana State University Press, 2000.

_____. *Cold Harbor: Grant and Lee, May 26–June 3, 1864.* Baton Rouge: Louisiana State University Press, 2002.

Sauers, Richard A. *A Caspian Sea of Ink: The Meade-Sickles Controversy.* Baltimore: Butternut and Blue, 1989.

Sears, Stephen W. *Landscape Turned Red: The Battle of Antietam.* New Haven, CT: Ticknor and Fields, 1983.

Sheridan, Philip H. *Personal Memoirs of P. H. Sheridan.* 2 vols. New York: D. Appleton, 1888.

Simpson, Brooks D. *Ulysses S. Grant: Triumph over Adversity, 1822–1865.* Boston: Houghton Mifflin, 1999.

Skelton, William B. *An American Profession of Arms: The Army Officer Corps, 1784–1861.* Lawrence: University Press of Kansas, 1992.

Small, Abner R. *The Road to Richmond: The Civil War Memoirs of Maj. Abner R. Small of the 16th Maine Vols.,* edited by Harold Adams Small. Berkeley: University of California Press, 1957.

Smith, William F. *Autobiography of Major General William F. Smith,* edited by Herbert M. Schiller. Dayton, OH: Morningside, 1990.

Stevens, George T. *Three Years in the Sixth Corps.* Albany, NY: S. R. Gray, 1866.

Stowe, Christopher S. "Certain Grave Charges." *Columbiad: A Quarterly Review of the War between the States* 3 (1999): 19–46.

Swinton, William. *Army of the Potomac.* 1866. Reprint, New York: Smithmark, 1995.

Tap, Bruce. *Over Lincoln's Shoulder: The Committee on the Conduct of the War.* Lawrence: University Press of Kansas, 1998.

Thomas, Emory M. *Robert E. Lee: A Biography.* New York: W.W. Norton, 1995.

Trudeau, Noah Andre. *The Last Citadel: Petersburg, Virginia, June 1864–April 1865.* Baton Rouge: Louisiana State University Press, 1991.

_____. *Out of the Storm: The End of the Civil War, April–June 1865.* Boston: Little and Brown, 1994.

U.S. War Department. *The War of the Rebellion: A Compilation of the Official Records of the Union and Confederate Armies.* 70 vols. in 128 parts. Washington, D.C.: Government Printing Office, 1880–1901.

Wainwright, Charles S. *A Diary of Battle: The Personal Journals of Colonel Charles S. Wainwright, 1861–1865,* edited by Allan Nevins. New York: Harcourt, 1962.

Williams, Kenneth P. *Lincoln Finds a General.* 5 vols. New York: Macmillan, 1949–59.

Williams, T. Harry. *Lincoln and the Radicals.* Madison: University of Wisconsin Press, 1941.

_____. *Lincoln and His Generals.* New York: Alfred A. Knopf, 1952.

Woodworth, Steven E. *Beneath a Northern Sky: A Short History of the Gettysburg Campaign.* Wilmington, DE: Scholarly Resources, 2003.

_____, ed. *Grant's Lieutenants: From Chattanooga to Appomattox.* Lawrence: University Press of Kansas, forthcoming.

Index